Clarity Beyond Stuck

How to Get and Stay Unstuck

Richard Elwell

Modern life runs at such a pace that we find ourselves with too much going on: countless different projects, to-do lists longer than your arm. We worry about money, family concerns and work deadlines. It feels like pressure, an unrelenting pressure imposed by future deadlines or an overload of information - all those emails collecting in the inbox, articles, book, manuals you are meant to have read. And with all this buzzing around in our heads it's often a nightmare trying to stay focused on what really matters.

You have decided that you can't go on working like this. But change can be tough. What gets in the way is contaminated thinking - worries, anxious thoughts and doubts - compounded by mistaken beliefs about how you 'ought' to be. The result is you end up out of sync with the ebb and flow of life. Past events, future prospects, other people's needs and demands are all mixed up, and this mish-mash can temporarily obscure your innate capacity for clarity, resilience and well-being.

It doesn't have to be that way. In fact it's quite possible to empty your mind of all the noise, untangle your thoughts and concentrate on what's important. The mind is a self-correcting system. We have a natural capacity for mental clarity, making connections, enjoying creativity and high performance. These 'factory settings' for confidence, clarity and self-belief are what you're born with. If you doubt this, spend some time in the company of a two-year-old.

Clarity Beyond Stuckness offers a way of cutting through that unhelpful clutter to foreground your wishes, dreams and desires, so that it becomes easier to determine which way you want to go. The first question many people ask when they hear about this is: "How do I develop that?" A better, more powerful question is: "What's getting in the way?"

Once you understand the process, then from now on, there are no excuses. And there will be no stopping you from achieving the best possible life for yourself and those around you.

Clarity Beyond Stuckness

How to Get and Stay Unstuck

Richard Elwell

Ethical Influence Ltd
www.ethical.influence.co.uk

First published by
Ethical Influence Ltd
Website: www.ethicalinfluence.co.uk

© Richard Elwell 2015

The right of Richard Elwell to be identified as the author of this work has been asserted by him in accordance with the Copyright, Designs and Patents Act 1988.

First published 2015.

All rights reserved. Except as permitted under current legislation no part of this work may be photocopied, stored in a retrieval system, published, performed in public, adapted, broadcast, transmitted, recorded or reproduced in any form or by any means, without the prior permission of the copyright owners. Enquiries should be addressed to Richard Elwell.

Ethical Influence Ltd has no responsibility for the persistence or accuracy of URLs for external or third-party websites referred to in this publication, and does not guarantee that any content on such websites is, or will remain, accurate or appropriate.

British Library Cataloguing-in-Publication Data
A catalogue entry for this book is available from the British Library.
ISBN-13: 978-1507880135
ISBN-10: 1507880138

Edited by Peter Young
Printed and bound in the UK by CreateSpace

Dedicated to Sarah, Toby & Ryan

Contents

Introduction   1
    Richard's story
    The story of NLP
    A place to contact your deeper issues

Part 1: The Past – Stories of Change   11
    Some case histories

Part 2: The Present – How people get stuck   23
    Different kinds of Stuckness

Part 3: The Future – What do you want?   45
    Outcome Setting

Part 4: The Cards – How to achieve the change you want   59
    Working with the cards
    Step 1 Write on the cards   61
    Step 2 Shuffle the cards   63
    Step 3 Observe   65
    Step 4 Decide which cards to keep   66
    Step 5 Tell the Story   69
    Step 6 Is that it?   71
    Step 7 Next Time   72

Conclusion   77

References   79

Introduction

This book is about getting unstuck and achieving clarity so that you can make the changes you want for your life and keep them. It's not just about dreaming and writing to-do lists. It's more 'hands-on', which means you are going to be actively engaged in clarifying your way forward. So let's start right away.

Jot down your first response to:

What are your three reasons for opening this book?

-
-
-

How my life is right now …

How I want my life to be …

What's different about this book?

Well, first of all, it's not different in that it asks a question that people have been asking for thousands of years. That question is: How do I really get what I want? You know, there's something about your life at present that you don't like, or don't want, or something you clearly want to achieve but don't know how. These are the kind of issues this book covers. You might think that by now we would have discovered a simple, straightforward way of doing this. It's true there have been lots of claims, and over time many solutions have been proposed. What I have found – which works well – is a way of doing this that when you know about it, it is kind of "Duh" obvious, but it's not the way we usually do things.

What this book is not

Before we get down to business, let me clarify what this is not about. Many books promise a 'quick fix'. Although that might seem desirable, the reality is that much as we would like them, there are no short cuts. A quick fix – if there were such a thing – would have little lasting value. It takes time to make deep changes. The method described in this book will take your time; it is not a Band-aid. You have to do the work. Just reading about it will probably do very little to change anything in your life. So, no short-cuts.

All change techniques will work to a greater or lesser degree – the key factors being your honesty and openness, how much you put of yourself and your energy into creating what you want. Change requires sustained work – grit – on your part. And it's ongoing.

Although some people can achieve a great deal off their own bat, trying to change on your own can be a challenge. You think you know yourself pretty well, but some things about you are so taken-for-granted that you cannot see them. That's where a skilled helper is useful; change is easier when you have someone there to help you. What makes the difference is another pair of eyes – a different point of view, a more objective point of view. You need someone who sees things that you don't see: your prejudices and blind-spots. We all hide things from ourselves, carry a degree of misinformation about who we are, what we are like, what we are good at. Some would say that we are all liars – especially about ourselves – but it would be fairer to say that there are some things that others may notice that we do not acknowledge for ourselves.

Once you become aware of what you're habitually not noticing – the elephant in the room, if you like – you can begin making real change. Now a book is a poor substitute for a real live person working with you. But I will do my best to provide the kinds of questions and observations that a coach or counsellor would offer, based on my experience of working with hundreds of clients.

> The you that you are familiar with is probably more 'surface' than 'deep'. There's often a reluctance or a kind of barrier that stops us going too deep, and so we back off. Other people can see these things about us – we are all skilled at reading between the lines when summing up other people. But ourselves – No way!

The first part of this book is more about achieving a 'data dump' of everything you know or think you know about yourself, so that you can examine exactly what is there. That means doing the 'impossible': noticing what you do not normally notice, acknowledging the elephant, becoming aware of what you are not normally aware of. But this isn't just 'data', separate bits of information. Human beings have the remarkable capacity for organising data into meaningful patterns and stories. Stories are basic: they condense huge amounts of information into a manageable chunks. We like stories, we tell stories, especially about ourselves. But stories are stories – they're easy to tell, but they are always distortions of the truth – often made more dramatic, because that's the way we like them.

The method described in this book works with these stories we tell ourselves, in a unique way. Instead of telling them to others, you are going to tell them to yourself. This in itself has a profound effect; confrontation can be very revealing, "OK, that's who I am." The real question is "Who would I like to be?" What other stories would you rather be telling? That's where the Cards come into play, and these are described in detail in Part 4.

Essentially, you'll be writing down key details of your life on small blank cards and then arranging them on a table so that you can literally stand back and see them from a different perspective.

Here we have the essence of what this book is about. It seems simple, and it's probably something you've never thought of doing before – it is different from writing a To-Do list. By reading this book, you will learn how to use the cards effectively, so that you can bring the changes you want into your own life.

Before that, let me tell you my story, so you can see how this all came to be.

Richard's story
How I got into this business

Looking back I can see it stemmed from being bullied as a child. I really needed to understand that because it became a pattern which progressed even through work. I never got on very well with people in authority or with people who had power over me. I joined the Scouting movement, and this was the first place where I encountered the power of leadership and training. It was the beginning of my way out of this. With the benefit of hindsight, how much easier it would have been for me then if I'd been able to go through this process that I now do.

But it wasn't a cure-all. Stuff like that hangs around and affects your life. I was able to find more success on the outside, but inside, well, that didn't get at the underlying discomfort. For a while I went into therapy. That was an eye-opener and I got a lot out of it. As time went on, I decided to train to be a facilitator. There was plenty of choice then as now. Part of what I found out, my learning from experience, was which were blind alleys, and how *not* to do certain things.

At that time in the UK, I was doing various leadership training courses, with the aim of working out how to get leaders more child-centred in their approach, to look at what they wanted children to learn and how to make the learning mind friendly to them. Then I went off to the States where I was listening to people whom you would have called New Age Thinkers: Skip Ross, Zig Ziglar, Tony Robbins, Shakti Gawain and Dan Millman.

I read about the family therapist, Virginia Satir, and really enjoyed watching videos of her working with families, which was occasionally highly amusing, but at the same time, what she was doing was awesome. A friend suggested that I do NLP, but I resisted because I thought it was just boy's toys and I didn't want anything to do with that. But Satir was influential in the beginnings of NLP, and later, when I did study NLP, I was able to deconstruct some of the really cool stuff that Virginia Satir was doing.

That led in a roundabout way to studying conflict management, and hypnosis, where I met somebody who suggested that I work with Michael Breen. That took me then, quite naturally, into learning NLP as a Business Master Practitioner. There was something so cool about Michael's work which I really enjoyed. Michael's initial response was, "I'll teach you the basics." I ended up spending a lot of time with him, and ultimately to where I am now. Michael's style of work will always remain a powerful influence. When I started the master practitioner training, it was because I wanted a ticket, a form of credibility. I came away with so much more. Michael would say, "Do you know what master practitioner means? It means you practice harder than everyone else." I've taken that to heart.

The story of NLP

At one time, NLP was flavour of the month. In recent years, NLP has had something of a bad press – in some cases deservedly, as it was being used in inappropriate settings in ways it was not designed for. Some of the claims made by many NLP people were exaggerated, based not on research but more urban myth. So NLP's credibility took a knock, and suffered the fate of the baby and the bathwater. Unfortunately for many, it has been dismissed out of hand by those who never discovered what it was for or how to use it effectively.

Let's go back to the origins of NLP and look at what it does well. Essentially NLP consists of a number of techniques, quite varied in style, which are used to undermine a fixed view of reality. People create their own particular model of the world based on their own experience (personal), on information provided by their friends and acquaintances (the social) and by the environment they live in (context). Over a life-span we develop and modify our beliefs about reality, how the world works, how other people are, and so on. Some of these beliefs become solidified as time passes, others fade away or change to some extent. However, some beliefs are 'sticky' – they hang around but no longer serve any purpose, and they may be tricky to identify. These are the beliefs that lead to a person feeling 'stuck'. This means that their model of the world, the meaning they are making of their experience, no longer offers any forward progress or action that appeals to them. They have reached a dead-end where no direction beckons. If you knew what to do, you would have already solved the problem. This is where outside help becomes useful. Using the tools of NLP it's possible to 'dismantle' someone's constructed reality, so that they may reconstruct it in some other way which makes sense to them. Such a reconfiguration or creative solution offers a way forward; the person now realises that they do have choices, and can achieve the goals they desire.

Changing your view of the world can be quick – the "Aha!" moment – but these are rare, and remembering your plan even harder. With any change, there is likely to be resistance – it means losing something of what in the past felt safe and secure, even though in many instances it felt bad. Better the devil you know, as the saying goes. Sometimes, a quick demolition job will work, but there are no guarantees that the person will be able to do much with a heap of rubble. It's better to take a little more care in dismantling, and then rebuild based on some kind of blueprint or plan. That usually helps. Though, as with any plan, it needs to be flexible and adaptable in the light of what actually happens once the person begins to think and act differently. Each change or adjustment will have knock-on effects that will alter their relationships with others.

> Old patterns die hard. People have been known to say "I just wish I could go back to such-and-such a time" – but what would be the point of that if they hadn't changed something of themselves first? The status quo has one major quality: it feels safe.

In practical terms, NLP offers a huge range of possible interventions. A practitioner needs to have multiple ways of bypassing resistance, of undermining someone's way of seeing their world, getting past their barriers. Now, you might think it necessary to help someone rebuild their reality, but this is something we all do anyway – we're experts at rebuilding. What we do need help with is rebuilding in a way which will be to our advantage; you need some kind of plan for the way you want your future to be different. There's little point in simply reconstructing a life just like it was before – you already know that doesn't work.

Stop living in the Past

A place to contact your deeper issues

I hope this has whetted your appetite! Although it sounds daunting, once you get going, you'll find you really get into the process and benefit greatly from it. So let's have a brief look at the practical considerations.

- *Do you need to tell other people what you are doing?*
  That's very much up to you: how much you tell them – because they're going to be curious, and they are going to notice differences. It's tough trying to do this with the people you are in frequent contact with – they have an investment in keeping you the same, because they have learned to live with that you. If you change, they'll have to update, and there's often a natural resistance to doing this. There is also a tendency for other people to try to undo changes in you, because it makes them uncomfortable. Be aware of this.

- *Do you need a special place to do this?*
  You will need some space, and a table. But it doesn't have to be special, just a place where you will not be disturbed for a while, a safe space in which to address your issues. Best not to have too many diversions available, such as computers, or phones. No multi-tasking; you need to concentrate on doing this. A space where you can focus on yourself, where you have time to go deep. A space where you won't be interrupted, where you won't be told "That's ridiculous" or worse.

- *How much time will I need?*
  This is time for you, and you do need to set aside sufficient time. You won't be doing this process in one session – you need time to pause, take stock, to 'sleep on it'. You will need to get some distance at times so that you can reflect upon what you have been discovering.
  There's no reason why this can't be fun, too, as long as you're able to step back without getting too emotionally caught up in what was probably quite stressful.

- *Do I work alone?*
  This is something for you to work out. The challenge of doing this kind of work on your own is that it's hard to push yourself hard enough. You are probably very skilled at not doing this, of avoiding rather than going through. So this really depends on how willing you are to dig deep into your own life and feelings.

It's vital that you do the actual work of writing and sorting. However, if there is someone you trust, who possibly has had some experience of coaching* or NLP who understands the importance of not getting 'sucked into content', then by all means have them present. They can ask questions, spot when you are avoiding something, and can keep you on track. This is useful but not essential. For example, it's very easy to cop out, and say "I don't know" to any question. There's lot going on behind a 'don't know' and it takes care and patience dismantling what is getting in the way of knowing. We'll look at being stuck in Part 2.

> Remember that the more you put into this, the more you'll get out of the process described in Part 4.

- **What do I need to work on?**
  You might want to improve your health, change your eating habits, be thinner, or stop smoking. You may want to work on relationship problems.

  Or you may want to improve yourself, progress in your career or generally in the world. You want to learn something new which is currently outside of your perceived comfort zone, something that you've watched yourself repeatedly failing at, or something where you've been good, but you need to be at the next level in order to be a success. This is not just remedial, but achieving higher performance.

  You may not have a specific idea at the moment, so you could see the process as clearing out the clutter, as priming your pump, essentially.

*   I prefer not to use the term *coach* any more as it has become over-used in the last decade. Instead, I call what I do Personal and Business Transformation.

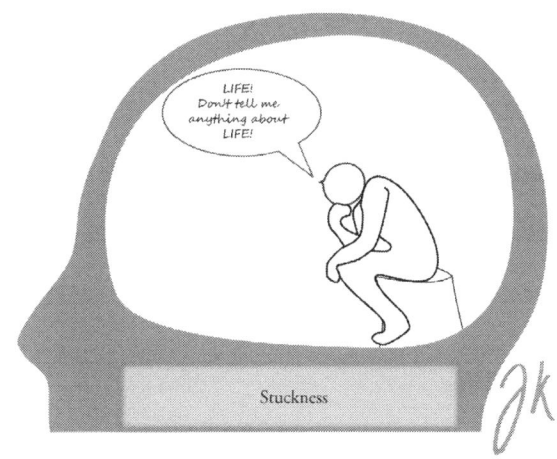

Below are some hints and stories which may give you some more specific ideas, so you can say, "Yes. I can see now. This is where I am stuck."

- ***What attitude should I adopt?***
  I invite your *benevolent scepticism*. Regardless of your level of competence, adopting this attitude allows you the opportunity to review your life as a complete thing.

> We see our lives as a journey along a path.
> You don't know where you want to be unless you know where you've been.

Life's Path

One metaphor we frequently use is to see our lives as a journey along a path. Wherever you are right now, you can look back and see the path you had trodden to get this far. You know where you started, and have a pretty good recall of what the earlier parts of your journey were like, and recognise paths which you chose not to take. And then turning, you imagine your current path continuing, but it's probably a bit hazy, because it's not happened yet. Your aim is to reduce the haziness by gaining greater clarity. There's a basic principle here: *you don't know where you want to be unless you know where you've been.* And starting from here, the next question is: *"Where do you want this path to lead you?"* You have probably looked forward and created a fantasy version of what you think you would like the rest of the path to be like. You might be quite definite that "I know what I *don't* want it to be like!" That's a start, but it's more useful to have something positive to go towards: it's more attractive, and you're more likely to achieve it.

In Part 3 we'll be look at this is more details, but you might wish to hold these questions in the back of your mind:

- *Which actions in the past caused you to follow this pathway that you're on now?*

- *Where do you want this pathway to lead you?*

There is a strategy, a trick that was taught to me, quite a number of years ago by someone who I respected. He asked two questions, one at the beginning of the workshop and one at the end of the workshop. And he asked people to write down their answers.

At the beginning of the workshop he said, "if you had the chance to ask the person that you respected the most, any question at all, what would that question be? Write it out. … OK. Now put it aside."

Part 1 : The Past – Stories of Change

The mind writes cheques the body can't cash.

The first part of the book is about where you are right now, and that's based on your past, the story of your life. This begins by you providing answers to the questions:
- Why am I reading this book?
- What is it about my life that I'd like to change?

How did you get to where you are right now?

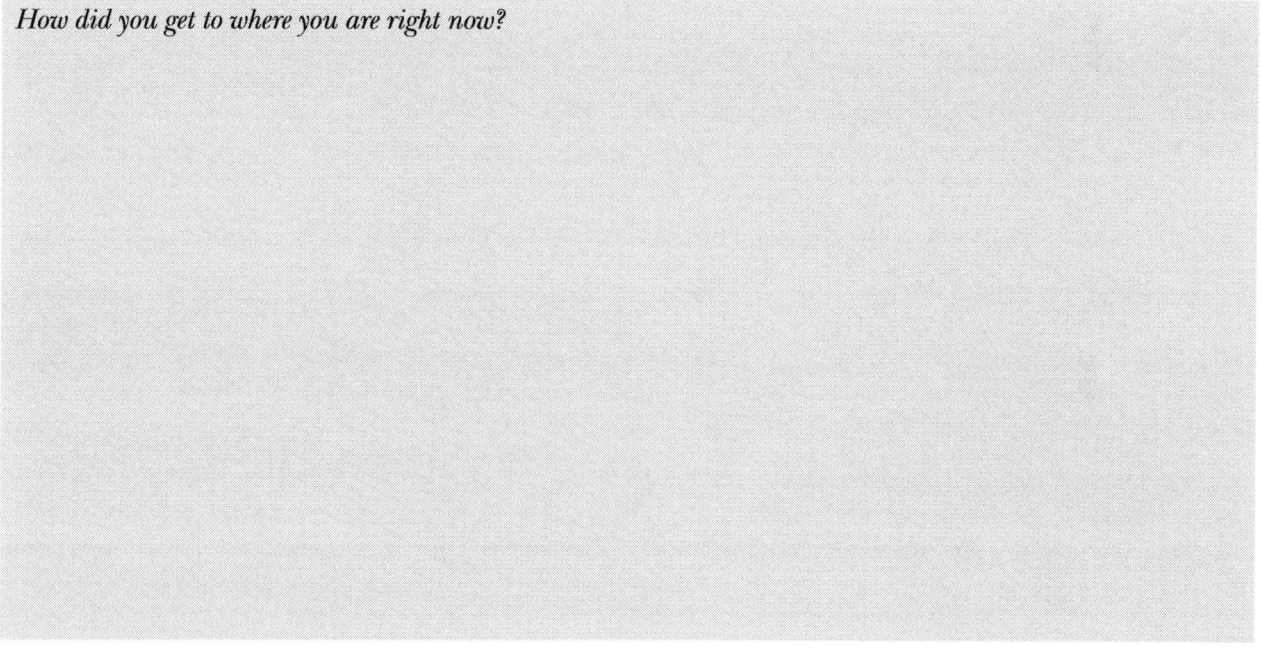

    Let's start by looking at the past in terms of the story of how you got to here. Just bring to mind that story you tell people about yourself when you meet them for the first time – the 'safe' version. Then, when you get to know them a bit better, you might divulge some more intimate details, your likes and dislikes, personal things that happened to you in your life that made you who you are today. All that stuff you have said dozens of times. You're probably tired of hearing yourself saying it!

    Now begin to fill in the details – the stuff you don't usually tell other people. This is for your benefit, and however cringe-making it is when you think about it, keep it to yourself. It's your personal history, but it's relevant to the journey you're about to take, because the aim of this chapter is for you to reach the conclusion: "This is me. Now. Warts and all." You may not like this picture of yourself, but it is a reasonably accurate perception of where you have got to in your life so far. As you continue to build up that picture by exploring your past, you're noticing those events and experiences that have had an impact on you. The thing is, this story now seems to be getting in the way of you moving forward. So that's what you're going to working on in Part 4 – rewriting that story so that it will serve you in future.

> You can only rewrite the story of your life, once you know what that story is.

The Sunk Cost Fallacy

Of course, when you examine the decisions you made, you may conclude, "Well, I've wasted my life; I've made a complete mess of it!" or some such negative self-putdown. But that is not a useful way of thinking; it's an example of the Sunk Cost Fallacy. That's the decision to invest further resources in something which is failing when there are better options open to you. It's when people stay in relationships or jobs when they would be better off out of them. Actually, when you look back at your life, you will see many activities which you once thought were a good idea – a particular relationship you wanted to initiate or make work but went nowhere, a business opportunity you were offered but turned down. Look around at the evidence of past decisions: the expensive golf-clubs cluttering up the garage, the subscription to the gym, or to a magazine you no longer read. Life can be full of regret. You could give the clubs away, or cancel the subscription, but that would seem like a personal failure.

> Not every plan succeeded – but you learned something from it.

A better way of thinking about these events where you have invested time and money, is to see them as 'your personal education course'. You were learning, and the best way to learn is to do lots of things and see which are worth continuing with. In the process, you undoubtedly found many that weren't worth the effort. Life is about making 'mistakes' and learning from them, and thus enriching your life experience. The better you get at this, the better you will be able to transfer your learning to new situations. Sounds easy, but it isn't – just tally the same mistakes you made over and over! (Not again!) Now imagine for the moment that you had led a 'perfect' life where you never made any mistakes. (Oh, the boredom of it!) Then comes a new and unfamiliar situation, where you are not sure what to do. However, there is no one else to guide you, and you are fearful of getting it wrong. And that leads to inaction.

It's all stories

We understand and explain our lives in terms of stories – ones we tell ourselves as well as occasionally telling others. A story 'makes sense' but it is always a simplification – because in order to generate a logical cause and effect sequence, many things which could have been part of the story are left out because they don't fit the particular version you want to tell. You don't mention some abandoned paths because you're a bit embarrassed about them.

We create our life stories by looking back – after the event, and with a particular bias. Maybe you're a glass half-full person, maybe half-empty ... And then you pull out the outstanding events – the ones with the strong emotional charge – and find supporting evidence for creating a rational explanation of 'what happened' and what it meant for you. Selective memory is a wonderful thing. It allows us to 'edit' our life into a story that feeds into our sense of self, as well as the way we present ourselves to other people.

> We are all used to editing our life-story. Now it's time to edit the past in order to create the future you want.

We need the world to be a certain way. Uncertainty is unsettling, so we find ways of stabilising the world so as to make any fuzziness as short-lived as possible. That's what stories do. However, one danger is that as soon as something becomes fixed, especially if we have given it a title or name, it takes on a kind of pseudo-existence. We think we understand the world, or that event, relationship or person. But the reality is, that was just one way of seeing it, just a point of view.

So let's have a look at some life-stories to see how individuals made sense of them.

Benedict's Story

Benedict had multiple issues. Over time he had developed a kidney problem and needed an operation. However, approaching the hospitalisation date, to make things worse, he had fallen from a horse and damaged his hips, so that he couldn't walk. At that point in his career, he was running his own business, but he had become very driven and had lost sight of where he was going. As such, he didn't know whether he wanted to run his business anymore, and because of his injuries his inability to act was turning into frustration. His focus had switched from business to personal.

It may seem obvious, but when you suffer and get to the point of nearly dying, your whole outlook on life itself changes. Whereas before, his identity had been closely tied up with his work, now he was no longer certain of who he was. Everything he knew himself as – his personal story – had changed. Before he'd been somebody who had had high energy and who got everything done straight away; now he was angry and had lost his purpose. He became confused and couldn't see a future for himself nor any direction to take that would provide illumination in his gloomy state.

I met him via an online questionnaire, which indicated his personality profile. What came out of this was his sense of hope. That was going to be enough to carry him forward into his unknown future. In the process, he would gain a sense of clarity and purpose.

Hope is a good thing to start with. At first he didn't know where he could go. He knew that he couldn't be who he had been up until then, because his body wouldn't allow him to be that any more. To put it simply, he was stuck.

So we sat down together and started working with the cards, and as we did this, even though it was initially quite painful for him to look at all these setbacks and what his life was like, he began to change. Having written things down on the cards he placed them on the table. I use a circular table which has a join, a line down the middle. I deliberately turn it so that when clients are working at the table that line stretches straight out in front of them. This, in effect, divides the past on the left from the future on the right of the table. What stood out for Benedict was that he had put down a majority of the cards to his left, because he was talking about the past – and much of it was quite painful.

The Footballer's Story

Jake was a footballer, who played for an Under 21s side. A left footer, which made him valuable. His cruciate ligament had snapped. His club sent him out to the US to get it fixed. They spent an enormous amount of money to get it done. But one thing they never bothered to acknowledge was that for any footballer or any sports person, if you're a left footer, when your cruciate ligament in your left leg goes, they fear that happening again. It's a profound fear. Even when somebody tells you that it's fixed, your brain knows that it could happen again.

Another footballer asked me to see him. Jake went through the process and came to the point where he was able to look back and say, "I don't know why I don't want to play." The utterance just tells you everything. But Jake just thought of this as rhetoric; he wasn't really listening to it.

I asked, "What was it like when you went in to the tackle?" That was a painful moment that he relived. I think that it wasn't just the pain, so much as the loss of what he thought he was going to become. He'd inherited that vision from his father who had frequently suggested he was going to be just as driven as he was. Now he felt like it was taken away. This is true of all change – there is always a sense of loss. It could be a lost part of your identity, or the loss of opportunities that will forever be closed to you thereafter. And for Jake, it had gone once. Even though it had been fixed, it was still breakable given a powerful kick or a hard tackle. So he backed off.

Subconscious takes the role as selfprotector

As a result, he was no longer in the same level of league as he might have been. For him, it was always in his mind to just play with the old rule that said 'if it happened once it can happen again'. Is this something he's really going to put to the test? No. It's about caution, despite the number of doctors telling him that there's more strength in his cruciate ligament now than there was before.

Most sports people, footballers, athletes, tennis players, when they go into any kind of competition they think of themselves as invulnerable or invincible. When you get injured, your perspective of yourself and your vulnerability changes. Doubt creeps in.

You could say that on the inside, something similar is going on: your unconscious mind's role is to protect you, to keep you from harm, and that may be something you're not aware of. The unconscious is turning around and says, "Whoa! Hang on baby! We had a really bad time last time you did this and you haven't proven to me that we're fine. I'm going to run the rule that says No Stupidity because I'm here to keep you safe and that's going to keep us from going to hospitals."

The Recruitment Officer's Story

Ann was in the recruitment business, but somehow she was recruiting the wrong people. The other people on the board were aware of this, and they had come to realise that she was not being the leader she needed to be. She was meant to be managing other people, but in reality, she was not holding people accountable for their actions, because – and this is the key point of this – she was afraid that they might come back at her and argue with her. Argument was something she was not willing to deal with. The business was approaching a state of crisis.

This avoidance came from her childhood. Her parents had decided that Ann's home life was going to be 'nice', and that meant that she would not exposed to conflict between them. Now, as we know, every relationship has moments of conflict, argument, fights, harsh words – but in any well-regulated household, there is also the reconciliation, the making up, apologies, the tears, the comforting hand extended. Because Ann had not been witness to this aspect of human life, she was the worse for it. Every child needs to see such situations resolved in a good way, not have them hidden, or shoved under the carpet. For Ann it meant that she avoided potential conflict in her work situation. And as you know, the work environment is a hotbed of discontent, conflict, opposing views – which managers are meant to sort out. That's why Ann was worried about the future of her job. Once word gets around that the business is failing, funding gets withdrawn, and so on, and the business goes down the tubes. Fortunately, things had not progressed this far, but if nothing changed, it undoubtedly would.

What Ann needed was to become the powerful person she could be. But this was not about her 'getting permission to be the boss' – which was how it came across when we were first discussing things. To sort things out meant going back to her childhood experience, and finding a better way of making sense of her mother's best intentions, which were not to sabotage her (although that is what actually happened) but to support her in growing up. It is very easy for those in power to impose their values on others, without thinking through the long-term consequences, even when they think they are acting in the other person's best interests.

We're going to leave Ann here, and catch up with her again in Part 4, when you have had time to think about how this story might apply to you, and you know a little more about the process of using the cards.

> Your habits have stopped you from evolving.

What to do with a story

Those stories are about people whose way of life has led them to a place of impasse. It's very easy to think we can jump in a solve the problem, or at least offer helpful advice. No. Don't do that. It's not effective and it's not helpful. Take a step back and give the other person the means and support for finding their own way forward.

Whatever the old story was, it no longer works, it's not relevant – circumstances have changed. One way of 'deconstructing' a story is to ask the questions:
- What does the 'hero' of this story need to learn?
- What are they currently not aware of?

It's also useful to know:
- How do they tend to mess things up?
- What 'bad habits' have they acquired?

What is it about habits? Perhaps you have realised that what you've been doing habitually has stopped you from evolving. A habit is a protective mechanism that allowed you to stay alive. I like to think that habits are often result from the work of your 'inner librarian'. Imagine there's a part of your unconscious mind which seeks order and stability, and who always puts things back 'where they belong'. Unfortunately, you come to believe that's the way things 'really' are. For example, you tell yourself, "I've been in a series of dysfunctional relationships. For some reason, I end up with the same type of person every time." So here is the challenge of looking back and going deeper, by being honest with yourself. Once you unearth the habit, the limiting belief, you realise: "Oh! No wonder I'm with that person." It's being able to self-reflect with honesty.

The Right Reasons

Make sure you're changing for the 'right' reasons. Looking back you may have noticed that you made decisions or life choices – job, marriage, etc – for the 'wrong' reasons, for WIIFM (What's in it for me?) reasons, rather than thinking in terms of What can I bring to the party, that will benefit not only me but the other people I will be relating to? Were you thinking that other people would supply what's missing in your life, rather than working to achieve balance within yourself?

This unknown need is something you are not consciously aware of, something hidden from you. However, other people can usually see it. This way of looking at things was described in 1955 by Joseph Luft and Harrington Ingham, and they combined their first names to create the Johari Window, sometimes referred to as the house with four rooms.

The Johari Window

There are four rooms or 'windows' which are of different sizes. Room 1 is the known world; it is the part of ourselves that we see and that others see. Room 2 is our blind spot; it is those aspects of ourselves that others see but we are not aware of. Other close friends may tell you things about yourself that you either don't see in yourself or deny exist. Room 3 is the most mysterious room in that it contains the vast unknown ... unknown to ourselves and to others ... the place of great danger and great opportunity. Room 4 is our private space that we keep hidden from others. The Known–Known Room 1 is much the largest. The whole purpose of going through the Johari window is to take the unknown which is unknown to you and unknown to the other person and make them bigger, make them better known. The rooms to concentrate on are the other three, and in particular, Room 3.

		Known to Self	*Not known to Self*
Kno	*Known to Others*	Room 1 The Arena	Room 2 The Blind Spot
Not k	*Not known to Others*	Room 4 The Façade	Room 3 The Unknown

Figure 1 The Johari Window

Exploring the past

Now it's time for you to think about your story, and how your beliefs about yourself fit into the four quadrants of the Johari window. There's no need to write anything down at this stage if you don't want to. What you need to do is to identify:

Identity

Recall the oft-told tales which you tell about yourself:
- "I'm ..."
- "I've always been ..."
- "People have always said that I'm ..."

You may see yourself as a person who is ... energetic or lazy, sporty, active, funny, depressed, sociable, a loner, maybe an entrepreneur or a leader, a follower or a worker, whatever.

Or you may think of yourself in terms of what you do: a carer, a helper, an analyst, a doer, a thinker, a creator ...

Or in terms of your relationships: a husband or wife, a parent, a son or daughter, a friend, a colleague, a team member …

Low points

Take care of yourself as you do the next bit, which is to think through the story of your life and pick out the black spots in your childhood, your teens, your working life – those things that are still with you after all these years, despite your best efforts to eliminate them. Forget 'mustn't grumble' – but make sure these are *your* low points, not just unfortunate events beyond your control. Watch your emotional state. If you are getting angry or depressed, take a break, do something different for a while. Remember that you survived whatever it was, and you're here to tell the tale.

- What are the 'dark spots' in your story? The things you wish you hadn't done, the embarrassing blemishes in your life you would prefer removed.
- What gave you cause to dislike yourself, or feel inadequate in some way?
- Identify any activities you still find yourself doing even though you know they're not in your best interests. For example, negative habits, fixations, addictions and so on.

If you're like the rest of us, it shouldn't be too difficult to come up with a substantial list! But be cool about it; it just means you're human. And because you're human, you can safely put these thoughts, these findings, away for the moment, so that you can move on.

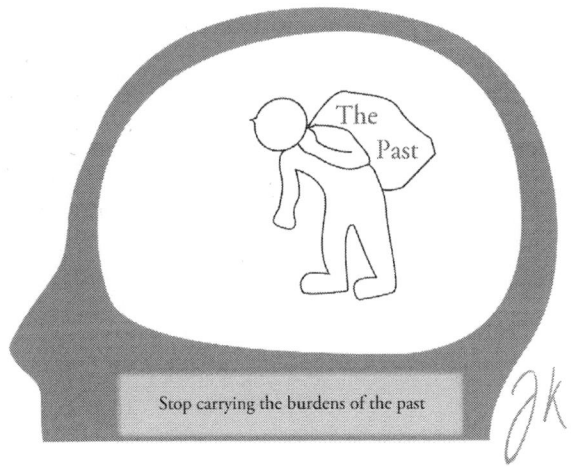

Stop carrying the burdens of the past

Reliving the Past

Life is full of repeats. In order to 'simplify' our memories of the past, we collapse them into soundbites, or condense them into oft-told-tales – these are the 'stories' that you come out with, given the right trigger. They're the stories that someone you know well, who's heard them all before, will groan "Oh, not that again!"

The more you tell them, the more they lose their spontaneity, but they may often increase in potency, in a negative kind of way. When you think about them, which you only do superficially, your attention misses the details, and only picks up the strong flavour of pleasure or regret. Alas, this oft-told tale can be easily mistaken for 'truth' – because it's become so simplified.

What happens to stories of the past is that they become iconic – set pieces, which you may even have given a title. You only need to think of the title, the cue word, the passing reference, and it all floods back. Well, not all, because the story has been pruned of many of the details which reflect badly on you. This story has been modified, probably in the direction of the primary emotion. Those which are positive, work now for the better, to your benefit – those of a negative slant become more so, and they become the reason for holding grudges, resentments, and regrets. When hear your cue you can once more relive the angst of some past wrong.

Even so, that story is about you in your past, and you and the world have moved on since then. Those stories need no longer apply, the context has changed, so do you really still need them?

Things to think about for Part 1: Stuckness

1. *You're reading this book because you feel stuck, and you don't know what to do about becoming unstuck. Start by describing your current feelings of stuckness.*

What does it feel like...

- *physically?*

- *emotionally?*

- *mentally?*

2. *How do you know that you are stuck? Describe what you are doing... or not doing... that you would want to do differently if you could.*

3. *How will you know that you are becoming unstuck?*

4. *What do you need to stop doing? Start doing?*

Part 2: The Present – How people get stuck

"In the midst of life's journey I found myself in a dark wood, for the right path was lost."

Dante's *Inferno*

Why do we get stuck?

This is one of the all time great questions. We get stuck because we can't see what we can do to make our situation better. Remember that definition of intelligence? It's what we do when we don't know what to do. Sounds good, but at times we all fall into the stupid category.

> Stuckness is not having options about what to do next.

Life has a tendency to provide us with the unexpected. Some of these events could have been predicted if we had thought long and deep about them, but we didn't. That's not human nature. We prefer to go with *If it ain't broke* ... not realising that it could easily get broke later, or simply run into obsolescence. Although we might quote *A stitch in time* ... we rarely get around to saving them.

Which means that we reach a point where we have limited our options, and no choice seems better than any other. We can rustle up a story which explains how we have got into this mess, this place of stuckness, but we cannot continue it into the next chapter: how to get out of it. In other words, the strategies we've been using have led us down a blind alley. So maybe the thing to do is to dismantle the alley, so that we can once more see possibilities open up for us. Could be brick by brick, or we could take a bulldozer to it ... Or we could remind ourselves that 'it's all in the mind' and then change the way we think about that story which holds our reality together, and then find a way of changing that. Then the blind alley dissolves into an open field.

In Part 1 we saw how some other people got stuck. It's very tempting to dive in and try to solve someone else's problem – because it's much clearer to us: "Aha, this is what you need. You did this wrong, you misunderstood that, and all you need to do is ..." Helping is a wonderful game, and much of what we do doesn't help, because we don't understand the principle of getting unstuck. It's not about offering 'solutions'; it's actually about deconstructing that particular story, that justification which holds them in stuckness. Trying to 'help' by suggesting "Why don't you ..." is doomed to failure because you're not changing the context. What's needed is something different, unexpected, for which the other person hasn't got a ready-made excuse for not doing it.

> Helping is not about offering 'solutions'; it's about deconstructing the story that's creating the stuckness.

Tell me about it

This chapter is for you to explore your own unique brand of stuckness. To help you do this, here is a list of statements that people often use to describe how they are stuck. You may find it useful to make notes, in whatever way you like. So let's start with some general businessy kinds of stuckness.

The Kinds of Business and Personal Sabotage Problems that Clients have
- I feel like a fake; it's like I'm only pretending to be a leader/manager, and someone is going to find me out.
- I don't think I'm in the right job – it's not fulfilling, I don't like the people, they bully me …
- I do my best, but somehow it all goes wrong. It's like I'm continually sabotaging my best efforts to achieve worthwhile goals.
- Actually, I'm not sure what I'm trying to achieve.
- All of the above.

One of the features of our storytelling is that it becomes too simplistic; we know that life is much more complex than a simple cause and effect. This is where an examination of where we are reveals a forest, not a single tree.

General
- *Lost their way in life*
- *Lack of sense of purpose*
- *Suffering from stress*

Health
- *Severe illness or disability*
- *Self harming*
- *Obesity, smoking*

Relationships
- *Breakup of marriage or partnership*
- *Numerous failed relationships*
- *Getting over bereavement*

Early years
- *Childhood abuse*
- *Bullied at school*
- *Parental divorce or separation*

Business and Employment

- *Business failure, couldn't see the way forward*
- *Decisions about the future of the business*
- *Couldn't sell, saw sales people as sharks*
- *Been made redundant and couldn't see a way back to employment*
- *Bullying at work*
- *Self destructive patterns, sabotaging personal success*
- *Lacking confidence*
- *Stressed out and told he would have a stroke if help not taken*
- *Poor management or leadership skills*

Other – *your particular problem(s)*

-
-
-
-
-

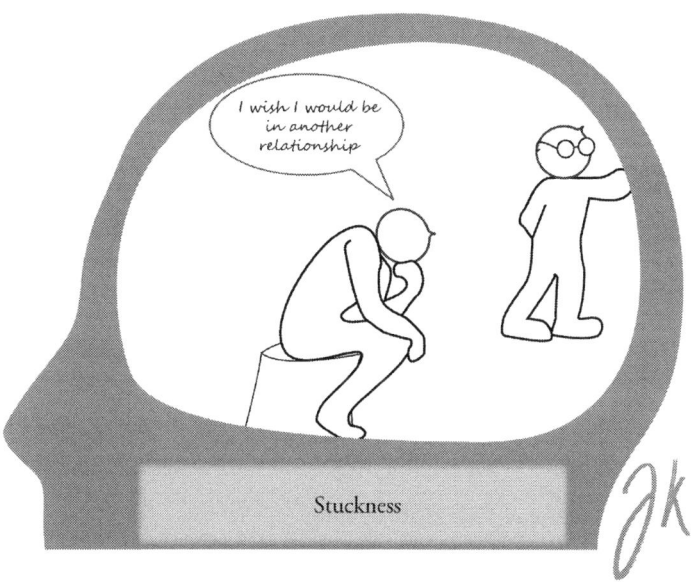

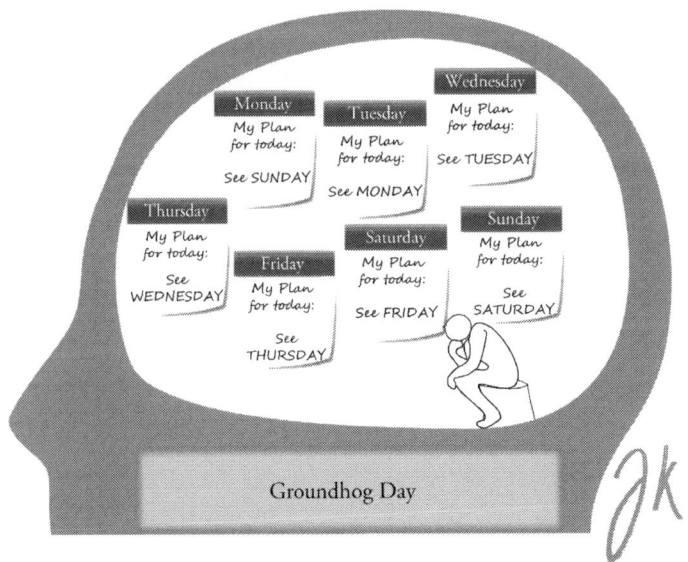

Groundhog Day

The benefits of 'having a problem'

You may not have thought of the upside of having problems, but this is something important to consider. If you hold for the moment the idea that whatever we do, we do for some purpose – whether or not we are aware of that purpose – then there is going to be some benefit we get from engaging in behaviour we describe as negative, undesirable, or that we wish we didn't do.

> Every problem has a benefit for you.

So recall a problem or issue that you think it would be worth doing something about. And then ask yourself:

- *What are the current benefits of having this problem?*

- *What does it allow you to do?*

- *What do you* not *have to do?*

And we can go a bit deeper, by asking:

- *What's your investment in having the problem?*

Think about all the things you have done, the money spent, energy expended, to get to this position in your life – courses taken, jobs done, all those things which you could consider as a cost.

- *Right now, what is your attitude to all that?*

Can you let it go, put it down to 'experience' or do you feel a burning desire to hold onto it at all costs?

There are some 'good' things about having a problem. For a start, it can be a way of defining some aspect of 'who you are'. A number of people who are suffering from some disability find that labeling themselves becomes part of their identity: "I'm dyslexic," or "I'm hopeless at maths." It's an excuse, it kind of assumes that no change or solution is sought – that's the way it is for all time.

Have you given yourself a label so that others treat you in a special way?
My labels:

-

-

-

Old habits die hard. If you're used to thinking of yourself as a no-hoper, a loser, a victim, then that's a reality you need to deal with – that's if you want to have a more interesting life where other things become possible. It's easier to play victim, because being a victim has its benefits. Therefore you need to find out what those are, because they may (or may not) be valuable. You won't know if they are worth retaining until you have had a good look.

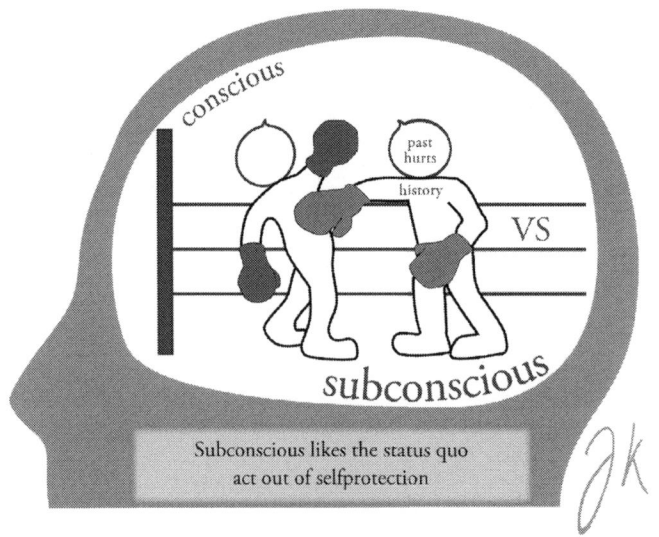

For example, it could it be a delaying tactic, or a signal for help, or a way of finding other people who share this 'problem' so that you can feel part of a group. Going on about your problem is a way of getting attention, or getting you sympathy. You may have noticed that a large proportion of the population delight in telling you their hard-luck or misery stories. Why do they do that? It won't make you feel better, so what does it do for them? Well, they have an audience, and it allows them to vent their anger or frustration, though that most likely doesn't change anything, and it's not intended to – they are maintaining the status quo: any change would mean behaving differently and that would alter their relationship to you and your colleagues.

If you're the one moaning and groaning, then people may feel sorry for you. They may even try to help you (a lot of people like to *feel* helpful) and then you can happily reject their help, because that makes you feel good or superior – and you'd rather stick with the misery you know than venture into the mysteries of changing.

On the other hand, you may be looking for someone to show you the way, to give you permission to change.

Do you need permission to change?

It could be you need to give yourself permission! Does that make sense to you? It could mean going against all those admonitions and pieces of advice you got from your parents or teachers – you know, those people who had your best interests at heart – and now getting in touch with the real you, and what you need to lead a fulfilling and satisfying life.

- *Whose permission do you need in order to be successful?*

You may also be in the middle of an extensive network of relationships and be influenced by these other people. After all, you don't want to let them down; you have to consider their feelings.

There are many ways in which you can be 'at effect' rather than 'at cause' in the world. So take a moment to explore the context you're in, map out some of the significant relationships. Notice the differential in status, which way the power flows: from you to others, or from others to you.

> Each of us lives in a reality which is constrained by our relationships. Sometimes this is good, but there will be also be 'toxic' relationships which do not benefit you. You may have considered getting out of these relationships, but something holds you back. Might be worth digging a bit deeper in that case and drawing up a list of pros and cons.

There's a point here which sometimes gets lost. It's because we observe other people's relationships and we ask, "How could you stay in that relationship?" It's because we're judging through our representation of what we think *our* life would be like in *their* shoes. But for them, that's their norm. That's what they do.

In a business context, there may be other kinds of constraints. The overall purpose is to make the business successful, and there may be those who hold to the notion that the end justifies the means. However, that is not a good rule for living, as it can lead to assaults on your values and the souring of relationships.

Some more questions to consider:

- *Who else is involved in decision-making?*

- *Are you the boss? Or do you need permission from yourself?*

Let's hear it for the status quo

Do you really want to change? It's messy, uncomfortable, you're going to lose something, and you'll have to reinvent yourself. Is that what you want? Do you want someone to come into your cosy world and mess it up so much that you have to change. "Oh no! I like the status quo!"

Subconscious likes the status quo act out of selfprotection

> People stick with what they don't want because it is 'known' and offers some degree of comfort. Whereas the unknown implies discomfort.

- What do you do or not do to preserve the status quo?
- Whom do you not want to offend, annoy, mess about so you keep stumm?
- Which elephants in the room are you unwilling to confront?

Think of that exercise where you have to imagine what you would save from a burning building: what are the essential things that you need to take with you? And what could be happily consigned to the flames?

The downside of change

You may feel the urge to avoid change, because failure or stuckness provides a 'safer' option. So, if you're threatened with change, one strategy is to retreat into what's familiar. In those situations you knew who you were, and you think now, erroneously, that you could go on being that you. Uh-oh. The moment you start thinking something different, you've blown that option. This is the Curse of Knowledge. Once you entertain that idea that things could be different, you notice that you're stuck, and having admitted it to yourself, there's no going back. Tough. Now you'll have to go forward.

> Because the future is unknown, it may feel unsafe. You cannot control circumstances, but you can be better prepared for whatever happens.

Creating a future always implies some loss of safety. It's unknown territory, however much you think you can control it. That's the deal. But scary can be fun – after all, what are funfairs and horror movies all about? But in your own life? Sure, you've done many things in your life without thinking through the consequences, and some of them worked out fine, didn't they? And if they didn't, you learned something valuable.

So looking back once more, consider:
- "Have you ever changed so significantly in the past that you thought 'I don't know that person I used to be any longer'?"

Even though you felt stuck at the time, something happened to unstick you, and you moved on. But because of life's complexities, it's not easy to see exactly what that catalyst for change was, nor easy to replicate it. If only you had a sure fire way of doing that ...

Well, now you do, and it's described in Part 4. This process has been tried and tested and found suitable for all kinds of stuckness.

Sorting out the Problems

You are becoming more familiar with those aspects of your life that you tend to keep out of sight – not just from others but from yourself. Bringing them into the open is a major step forward. The truth is, you've survived this far, so you must have something going for you! The secret of moving forward is to see clearly what that resource is.

Generally it's hard to make meaning of your life, your work, your relationships and so on, because it's all jumbled up in your mind, and it's hard to see things clearly because it's complicated. As you begin to untangle your reality, you gain clarity which enables you to make decisions about how to act, the best way to bring about the changes you want.

Think of the age-old metaphor of the wood and the trees. When you're in the forest, whichever way you turn, it's trees. One way out of this is to change your perspective: rising above all, that is a good way. Imagine you're in a hot-air balloon, getting higher and higher ... Now with your bird's eye view you can see the forest below and map it out, plot some paths leading out of it. Your imagination allows you to overcome the limitation of being stuck inside your brain by mentally getting your distance. This is easier done by physically standing back, and by dumping what's in your brain out on the table in front of you. No longer is all this stuff buzzing around in your head – it's there and you can see it. And the more you move further back, the more the feelings about it reduce. You get more objective, you gain clarity.

The metaphor I use in this book is putting the cards on the table – here, literally, you write your ideas, thoughts, memories, wishes on cards which you then put on the table in front of you. This begins to untangle everything, so that you get a clearer view of what's going on. It also means you can take sensible action as you're no longer so emotionally involved in the problem.

Subconscious takes the role as selfprotector

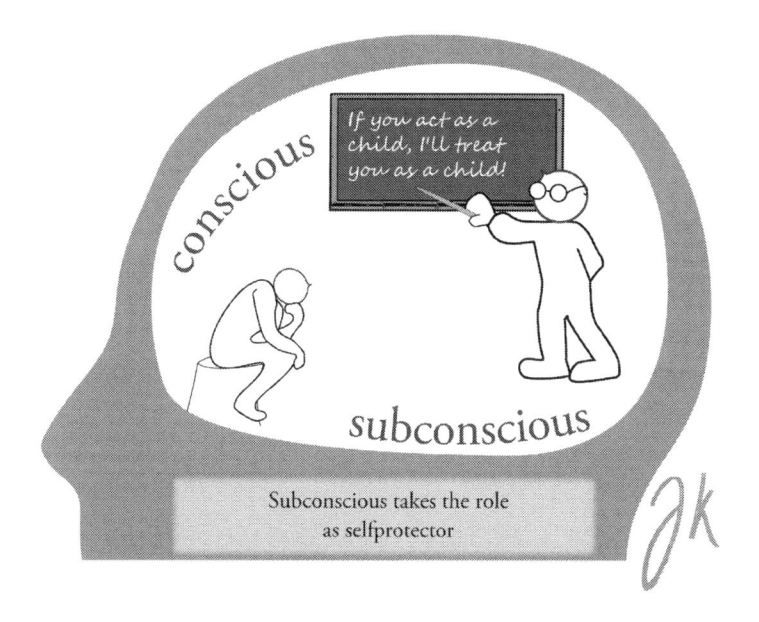

And you begin to see the story. In Chapter 1, I said that we make meaning of our lives by weaving stories from the events, emotions, encounters. When you're asked, you can easily put things together and construct a meaningful narrative. We all do this quite naturally. Changing your life means changing some of the stories, both changing what you already have, and by adding elements to create new stories that will initiate a path to where you want to be.

By working with the cards, you are going to find out how easy or difficult it is to make changes. You'll gain clarity: discover the underlying patterns, stories, beliefs, values that affect your current behaviour. You are the writer and editor, so it's what you do that will make a difference, will show you the next steps to take – your way out of the forest will become clear.

> We're used to making small changes, finding new meaning, telling new stories all the time.

Stories are not written in stone; they change according to need. A particular story 'stabilises' the world for a period of time – long or short – and you believe "This is the way things are." As long as this understanding is stable, it enables you to work out what to do next. As soon as you take action, the world changes in some way, and overwrites the previous version. It's so automatic, so in the background, that most of the time we don't notice. Why would we?

Spring cleaning

Maybe you don't need to change anything or do anything other than remove the accumulated stuff which is obscuring your view. Decluttering these topmost layers will reveal more of what's deep down, the 'truth' of the situation you find yourself in. Sometimes, just doing that is enough. Awareness brings enlightenment. It's like the Freedom of Information Act – ask the question, gather facts and that removes misunderstandings and confusion.

Maybe you're thinking this is for other people: They can do that. I've been trying all these things for years and look where it's got me! Or perhaps your recognise this condition in other people, because you're good at diagnosing other people's issues. If you can see where they are stuck, because that's 'obvious' to you, this could be holding up a mirror to how you yourself are getting in your own way.

If you assume that other people are also doing this, you could ask them to give you their ideas of what they see your stuckness is about. Ask:

- *How am I currently performing?*

If this is your business partner, your spouse or your best friend, what have they noticed? (Remember the Johari Window.) What is it that they will suggest that you are doing well? What will they suggest that you are not doing well enough? How do they think you are getting in your own way? What would they suggest is the key thing, which if you changed that, everything else would fall into place?

Stress management

You could even go one step further:

- *What would you say your current anxieties are?*

- *What keeps you awake at night? What is it that stops you from sleeping?*

- *How do you usually get out of this stressful situation?*

Stress implies that you are being asked to do more than you really want to do. You have to do things, but you think you'll not be able to cope, and this generates anxiety about the future. You fear that you'll not be able to perform to the level which is expected, appropriate, demanded, or to which you aspire. There are both internal and external pressures here: the fear of burnout, that if you actually do what's expected, you'll no longer be able to function at all!; and the threat of being found incompetent which brings the probability that you'll lose your job, or never be able to work again, at least, not in the same role.

What are your stress points?
- It could be money, workload, family problems, health. Be specific: What do you actually have physically wrong: irritable bowel, vomiting before going to work, your hair is falling out? Whatever.

- What exactly is the money problem? People usually claim that they don't have enough, but would any amount ever be enough? So find the right level.

- Other people have enough money to be able to do what they like, but they don't have their health. If you have a sick family member, then there is no amount of money that's going to solve that problem – something else is required.

- Money is really only a means to an end – so what might that end be? It isn't just to be able to sit in your counting house and run gold coins through your fingers. You want to be able to make some kind of change in the world – to your world. So what is it? What would you be specifically be doing with that money? Take holidays? Improve your children's education? Support a worthy cause?

Another question to ask is:

- *How bad does it have to get before you'll take action?*

We all need a little stress; it keeps us creative, on our toes. But how much is good for us? So before you try to remove it, consider: What we're doing is taking *dis*tress – the negative stress – and converting it into *eu*stress – which is positive stress. The level of pressure we need or can tolerate in our lives is very much a personal thing. What's common is that we need to be driven by stress in a positive direction. By laying out your thought process using the cards, and then rearranging them, it then becomes possible to see a pathway from distress towards eustress and a positive outcome.

- *Which are the key things which are creating stress or causing you to have anxiety?*

And:

- *What would the ideal state look like if you didn't have this anxiety?*

But don't think about that yet.

Perhaps by now, you are feeling really miserable! Oh dear, what to do? But this is not the time for self pity, or slumping back into denial – that being the fall-back position for many human beings. Instead of being energised to do something about it, they say, "I'm just going to be here and be sad because it's safe and comfortable. I don't actually have to take any action to change the way I'm thinking or to be in a different place." But that's not you. You have business to attend to.

So now, your story, your life story, has had some of the 'missing pieces' restored. These are probably not the 'nice' pieces you really want to think about. Never mind. They're essential ingredients in the story of you, and need to be taken seriously. Well, a bit seriously. Be nice to them, because they could soon be off.

That nagging voice in your head

The Call

You could think of what you've just been considering as a wake-up call, an invitation to recognise the story you are telling yourself, and to then let go of that story because it's served its purpose. It got you to this point right now when you're about to do something about changing.

Think about the Call. Throughout your life you are getting calls to action. Some you heed, others you ignore. It might be worth a moment or two to think about how this works with you.

- *How would you recognise the call to action? What has to happen? How strong or serious does it have to get before you'll do something about it?*

- *How do you usually respond to requests for change?*

- *What stops you responding? What tells you "No, not this"?*

- *Who gets in the way, who prevents you? Who says you can't do it? Who says you can?*

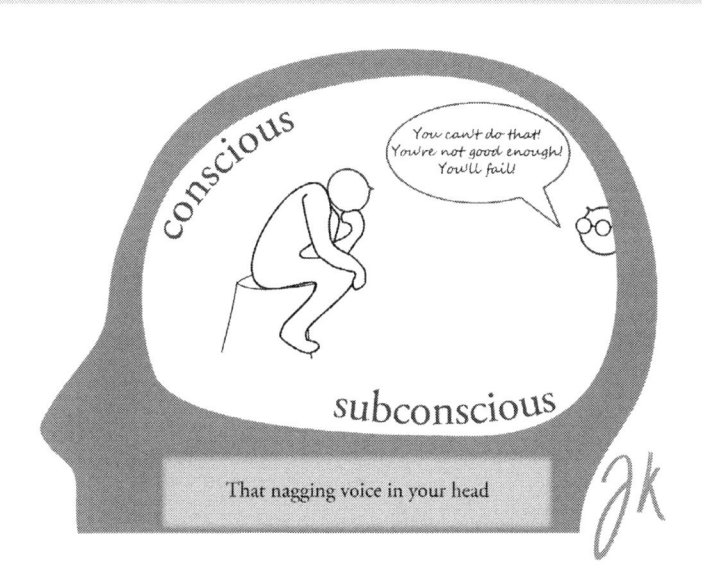

That nagging voice in your head

Who supports you?

It's tough making changes if the people around you are not supportive. Because once you change it disturbs their status quo and they do their best, often unwittingly, to return things to the way they were before. The known world.

- *Who has supported you in the changes you have made?*

- *Who are your cheer leaders?*

- *Who are your sayers of doom, your detractors?*

Sometimes the people you knock around with are genuinely helpful, sometimes it's superficial, and you guess some kind of hidden agenda. Beware the company you keep.

Some people you judge are being deliberately difficult, but later, looking back, you realise that they weren't trying to 'rescue' you, they were monitoring your progress to make sure you were on track, allowing you the space to learn and grow, because they knew you were capable of doing this.

We all need support and back-up from the people around us. So who are they? Write down their names for each of the contexts you find yourself:

At home:

At work:

At leisure:

- *Is the context in which you work – the organisation and its culture – going to support the 'new you' when you have changed and are doing more of what you want?*

- *If you change, who else – friends, colleagues, bosses, subordinates … – is also likely to change?*

Refusing the Call

What would happen if you were to do nothing? Changing is not compulsory, and there have been numerous times in the past when you thought it wasn't worth the effort. People say "I'm OK" or "I'm Fine" – but that's just an exchange of social pleasantries. It often means "I don't want to talk about it."

- When have you said "I'm fine" and not meant it?
- What are your (familiar) reasons or excuses for not having tackled this already?

Defensiveness has its place: you want to stay safe. You're simply protecting yourself. The process of change can make you 'fragile' or feeling vulnerable. You're not yet used to being the new you. So when you work with the cards, make sure it's your space, your time for doing it. Avoid the possibility of others mocking you. You need a place where you can negotiate with yourself without interruption.

> Make sure you have got other people's support before you start the change process.

Pulling this all together

OK, you've been delving into your past, the historical reasons that you find useful to explain why you are who you are at the moment. Let me put it to you: Here is the mess. It's your mess. So how do you relate to this mess?

What follows is not going to be all doom and gloom. It's looking for the bright spots. What are your good points? What do you think what you're good at? What have you done that you are proud of?

Make a note here of what you are proud of. These could just be the things that motivate you, provide the impetus for doing better ...

This is the beginning of seeing things from different points of view. If you can't immediately think of your good points, put yourself in the position of someone who knows you well. What would they say you were good at? If you're married or in a relationship with this person, what is it they see in you that means they want to be with you? You could always ask them. Seriously.

Things to think about for Part 2: The Present

1. *What do you think in your past has impacted you the most in terms of your ability/inability to move forward?*

2. *Who are the people in your past who have had the most impact on your current life?*

3. *How have they impacted you both positively and negatively?*

4. *Since the old theory says that past behaviours are the best predictors of future behaviour (which you will be able to change after working through this book), what past behaviours have you exhibited that you would like to change?*

Part 3: The Future – What do you want?

"The future depends on what you do today."

Mahatma Gandhi

Now we turn our attention to the future, and explore: "Where would I like to be and how am I going to get there?" This presupposes that there is a way out of your stuckness, that you will find it, and this is something you will discover for yourself.

Apart from contemplating where you want to be instead, you are asking yourself: "*Who* do I want to be?" because in the process of change, a transformation occurs, not just of what you *do*, but of *who* you are. As you change, your relationships also change – some for the better and some not. There will often be people who don't want to adjust to the new you, and your relationship with them dwindles. And by way of compensation, you will encounter other people who appreciate this new you, and relationships flourish.

The 'inner' Librarian

The Past — The Future

You know who you have been

Perhaps at the moment, thinking that it could all be different seems to be just a fantasy, or leaves you with a sense of blankness: I don't know who I want to be! Which is, of course, only natural, since you have yet to become that you.

> As you change, everything changes, including who you are.

On the other hand, when you answer the question: "What do you want out of life?" you can probably come up with something, though this may be something 'respectable' or 'safe' – what you think others might want to hear to say. Or it could be that there are so many things you want, you find it extremely difficult to choose any one of them as the main thing. Which one bobs up to the surface depends on your mood or what you've just been doing. This is where the cards come in useful. They enable you to record all these different aspects and options, so that you can then sort them out in your own mind. It's about prioritising, getting things in perspective.

> Getting clarity on what you want is not a one hit affair. As you move towards your goal or goals, what you want tends to get more refined, clearer, and will sometimes change completely.

Magic

I don't know about you, but I grew up with the idea that there's a kind of magic connected to keeping your wishes secret: "Blow out the candles, make a wish, but don't tell anyone what it is." It's like we expect something extra – just so long as we don't think about it – but we don't often admit this or make it explicit. In other words, we don't want "within operational parameters" – we want magic. Consequently, there is a kind of fear associated with telling our secrets – a belief that if we do make our wishes explicit, that will somehow destroy or negate them.

Do we really hold that what we actually want is what we *say* we want. Aren't we being just a bit 'modest', a bit disingenuous? What we really want is 'something extra' (we go to a concert and demand encores; we want Bonus Tracks, and Extras on the DVD) over and above our need or want, of what was on offer, was advertised, proposed … We really want to have a 'nice surprise', an unexpected bonus in addition to the well-specified, detail shopping list that we created in order to solve a particular problem. Why is this? Because getting exactly what we asked for wouldn't be much fun. We like surprises, odd twists that make life 'interesting' – even in the Chinese sense of living in interesting times.

Now it's time for making your birthday wishes, your hopes and dreams explicit. These desires need to be as realistic as possible – after all, you do actually want these things to come true, not remain forever unattainable goals. There's no need to be shy; it's time to get clear about your desires as well as those things you already have which are going to help you make them come true – your resources.

Glimpses of the future

Imagine that you're at the cinema, and you're just about to enter the auditorium. There's a narrow gap between the swing doors, and you can just make out some flickering pictures on the screen. You can't see the whole picture, but you notice at the far left-hand side of the screen there's a tiny image you can make sense of. And it gives you an idea of a possibility for your life – and just because it's a possibility doesn't mean to say that you necessarily have to make it come true. Don't reject it out of hand, but treat it with a sense of playfulness, a choice to be entertained. Most people lose hope when they think they don't have a choice, if they feel their life is pre-destined, the script is written. But that's not the case. You can say Yes to things and have an interesting life. Even if you choose not to make a choice, you have still chosen. And that brings us to a key point, which is that you are creating your life, and making the decisions (by default or not), so from now on, there is no value in blaming other people for you making poor decisions.

> You are the person creating your future. You cannot blame anyone else.

This is why a playful attitude is so important, and that's one of the purposes of using the cards, because like any card-game, it gives you time to explore, to try out possible moves, all within a set of rules and limitations. Life is not 'anything goes' with no restrictions. It is the rules and limits that bring out your creativity. Now, some of these rules were imposed way back, by your parents, your teachers, those 'significant others' in your life. They may have been appropriate at that time of your life, but that was then. This is now. Therefore you need to clarify what those rules are and decide whether you want to keep them, or whether to find a new set of rules to live by.

What do you want?

What are your hopes and dreams, your fears, your wants, your needs, your goals, how much money do you need, what friends do you want, what sort of relationship would you want, what sort of car you want, where do you want to visit …?

Think in terms of the big picture. Then go for the details. Not just the feast and the menu, but the ingredients and the recipes.

My hopes and dreams:

But steady on here. What you don't want is to try to micro-manage your future by specifying every single detail (unless you're in manufacturing or software development), because putting these limits on the future, you'd find that when you got it, you'd be disappointed.

- Think about means and ends, the intermediate steps to achieving the end result.

For example, you don't want the drill bit to make the hole, you want the hole so that you can hang up your picture. And you want to hang up the picture because ...

Have you thought it through to the end, or are you just working on something that will disturb the situation?

- Having thought through the details, go back to the new big picture: will it work?
- Make sure that what you want is within your gift. That is, it doesn't depend on someone else doing something or changing first – over which you have no control.

Make some notes about what you want:

A current situation needs to change
- *personal – body, wellness, fitness, your relationship to your physicality*

Your circumstances – job, money, relatives, your values, attitudes
- *context – relationships, job, location*

- *relationships – with your partner, your spouse, children, boss, team ...*

Something is missing
- *a comparison with others : what do other people have that I want, am jealous of?*

- *a need : "If I had x, then I'd be able to do y ..."*

Something's gotta go
- *Something is holding me back, limiting me in some way*

- *A negative or unwanted behaviour or response*

- *A dysfunctional relationship*

How SMART were you?

Much has been said, written and PowerPointed about outcome setting. Over the last few decades some of the mantras have become main-stream, which means they are now taught on business or management courses, and even in schools. Some of the ideas associated with setting SMART outcomes or other variations on the theme may be effective. One aspect is to change the way you think about the future and what you want by focusing on the what you want to move *towards*, rather than what you want to get *away from*. However, both should play a part of your deliberations. If you are the kind of person who sees life as half-empty, then switching your attention to the more positive aspects of life may be enough to trigger great changes in what actually happens. The main benefit is that you focus on the future, rather than bemoan the past. Because the future is 'open', you become more open to possibilities. If your past is a closed book, then you're stuck with it.

You might even find the following belief useful: "Trust that the universe is actually giving you what you want and need." See the world around you as mirroring who you are right now. Do you like what you see? Do you want to change anything? Chances are, you will want to.

If wishes were horses ...

It is certainly a good idea to clarify what you want, and where you want to be, but positive thinking – despite its promotion – is simply not enough. Just 'thinking positive' is sometimes counterproductive: trying to make yourself feel happy is often the very thing that makes you feel miserable. Sure, it's a good idea to make your desired outcomes SMART, or well-formed, or whatever, but more is required if you are going to increase the probability of achieving them. The something extra means considering the worst that could happen, and then putting in the effort to keep things on track. Just visualising yourself in some future reality with all the money, the yacht, the fast car and so on keeps you in the land of dreams. OK, have the dream, but then bring it down to earth. Get real.

> After a series of experiments designed to assess the effectiveness of having 'positive fantasies about the future', the German-born psychologist Gabriele Oettingen and her colleagues discovered that spending time and energy thinking about how well things could go actually reduces most people's motivation to achieve them. This is because the mind begins to think that the goals have already been achieved, and thus need not bother about them any longer. Oettingen suggests that a better strategy is to think ahead about all the possible challenges and downsides of going for that particular outcome.

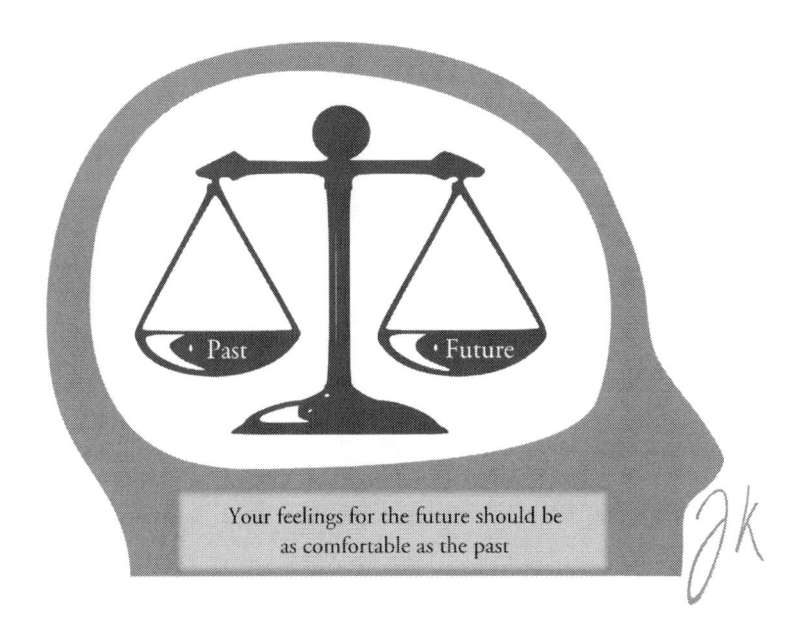

Your feelings for the future should be as comfortable as the past

Both sides now ...

The mistake people make is assuming that visualising the goal as already achieved is enough. Not so. If the mind thinks that the goal has been reached it powers down the desire to actually get on with the physical challenge of making it so. The challenge has gone. So what you need to do, having dreamed your fantasy outcome, is to then use your imagination again to think through all the obstacles to reaching it, the things that could go wrong, or the aspects of that outcome that you wouldn't like (maintaining the boat, finding crew, seasickness, insurance, security, and so on).

When you look at these negative factors, you may decide you don't really want that particular goal after all. It's too much hassle. Or you might change your mind when you think of the hours of work ahead of you to actually fund this future desire, because you can't rely on winning the lottery, or becoming a world-famous singer. Having thought through these things soberly, and you still want the realistic challenge, then now you become motivated to get moving. Remember the saying: There's no such thing as a free lunch. A dream is just a dream – until you ground it. That's why you need to get realistic for a moment, and consider all the other factors you can think of, and the feelings that go with them.

Make some notes here about the obstacles you face:

-
-
-
-
-

No free rides
"No Battle Plan Survives Contact With the Enemy"

German military strategist Helmuth von Moltke.

Another factor is our inability to predict the future. We can't. Nothing works out as planned – there are always unintended consequences of our initial steps. Change is an ongoing process, not a one-off. As soon as one change occurs, the world is different, and the initial conditions no longer apply.

Expect the unexpected. Re-planning your next step into the future is ongoing.

Every intervention changes the world to a greater or lesser extent, and we assign a positive value to some consequences, and a negative value to others.

Consider: what are the costs entailed with actually getting what you want?

- What will you gain, and how will you accommodate these gains?
- What will you lose in terms of: things, money, resources, opportunities, people, friends, trust, respect …?
- Do you ever subscribe to the belief that you will strive to achieve your goal *whatever the cost, whatever it takes*?
- Do you believe that sometimes *the end justifies the means*?

Bear in mind the Warren Buffet principle[1] of stopping doing something in order to make way for the new you. You need to concentrate on the main thing, not spread yourself too thinly. You cannot continue filling up your life with more stuff, more purposeful activities. You need to prioritise, and that means letting go of what is not the main thing.

Follow the expert

Modeling excellence was the other original intention of NLP. If you want to know how an expert does something, study them in order to find out what makes them special. Again there are provisos on this. There are no short cuts. Experts became expert by putting in the practice. Although modeling experts is a good idea, if you only study what the winners did, you can easily be misled. The losers may have been doing something similar, and yet they disappeared from the radar. In many surveys of the good and the great, the losers are under-represented, and this biases the findings. Therefore, you also need to know what those deemed failures did – as there may be a deal of overlap – to identify what really makes the difference. If, as is often the case, the 'evidence' is based on self-reports, then this may be extremely vague and open to a variety of interpretations. And it will almost certainly exemplify confirmation bias. People justify what happened by writing a story that leads to the happy ending and everything that went wrong along the way has been conveniently pushed to one side.

> Success stories are been written by the winners, not by the losers.

Happiness is not a goal

There are many, many influences in our culture which suggest that happiness is the be-all and end-all of life. Sure, we all want to be happy. But setting that as a goal is ill-advised. Why? Because happiness is a state, and often it is a state which you only recognise after the event. Those things which bring you happiness are often those moments when you are totally absorbed in doing something; you're 'in the zone' or 'in a state of flow' – you don't have time to evaluate how you're feeling because that would be an interruption. If you think of happiness as being in a position where you are doing something whole-heartedly, then it would be better to focus on what those activities are, rather than the state you might possibly be in. As in *Hamlet*, It's all 'good' or 'bad' depending upon your point of view, your frame of reference.

> Antarctic explorer Ben Saunders[2] says in his TED talk, describing his journey to and from the South Pole on foot, "Happiness is not a finish line."

It's not finding the positive result, the 'event', that matters. What's more important is looking at how you responded, the action you took. What you do when you are faced with a novel situation.

Whenever one of my clients says "I want to be happy", I point out that the job is already taken – along with Dopey, Sneezy, Bashful and all the other Dwarves. OK. Do you really need permission to be happy? Why not choose to be happy now, happy that you are taking steps to sort out your future. There are several sayings in our culture about this: Count your blessings. Look on the bright side. And there are some things which when you think of them, will bring a smile to your face. "Always look on the bright side of life. De dum…" Yeah. So that's something not going to be on your list in the next part of the book, because you already know how to do that.

Writing the future story

> Life is a path that you beat while you walk it.
>
> Antonio Machado, *Proverbs and Songs, xxix*

The story is not yet written – because it is future oriented; the path does not yet exist (even though you think that past memories have provided you with stories which define a path – that the future will be pretty much the same as the past …). You are going to be developing the skill of creating new paths. You are coming up with options, not defining micro-managed certainties. You have a hope, a belief that what you desire is attainable. This hope is sufficient to motivate you to create your own path step by step.

As an example, think about planning a holiday. You can taken an 'easy option' and buy a package which someone else has organised for you – a package which has been tested with other people and has become 'safe'. Or you could be more adventurous and do it yourself. The internet helps; it reduces the time and effort. You decide on a location, hotel, price, amenities, and you look at other people's recommendations, and so on. You also have to work out how you are going to get there – using airports, trains, hire cars, and so on. You book. On the chosen date, you set off.

You don't have to have it all worked out ahead of time. It's never possible to do this. There might be delays, strikes, bad weather, cancelled flights. You probably won't want to think of such contingencies, but it's a good idea to be prepared for them – you know what it's like.

To reach your goal, you have to get in there, get your hands dirty, get your feet wet – there are many metaphors for this. It's not about being perfect, it's about getting on with it. And again, you will be meeting your need for 'surprises' – hopefully ones you will gain from, ones that will give you memories that you will fondly look back on.

The 'inner' Librarian

The Past   *The Future*

You know where you are going as well as where you've been

"Oh, No! Not Reality!"

It's also a good idea to have some explicit criteria that let you know that you've got what you wanted. With the holiday, it's easy. With the more abstract desires, you need to define some criteria that let you know when you've arrived. Otherwise, you could go on forever, feeling that you're not getting anywhere. For example, what would you understand by 'enough'? Enough money: what does that mean? Most people think they never have enough. Time to put it in real terms, give a figure. A satisfying relationship: how would you know? All relationships have their ups and down, so what would be a good indicator that your relationship was growing, evolving?

Here are some questions to consider:

- *How will you know you're successful? How will you know you've reached your goal?*

- *What does it look like, sound like, feel like when you're there?*

- *How would someone else be able to tell that you've achieved your desire? What would they see that was different about you?*

- *What will your friends be saying about you?*

It's also worth checking how you will be or feel once you have got what you say you want. So ask yourself, in relation to a particular outcome:

- *"So if I got that, would I be satisfied?"*

- *"So if I got that, and just that, would it be enough?"*

Imagine that you now have what you said you wanted. Is it really enough? Is it more than enough? Are you content, or does it just open up a gap which will need other things to come along and fill it?

Motivation

By now, you might be sufficiently fired up to want to get on and start making changes. If you are, good. Proceed to part 4.

If, however, you still need a bit of a push to get going, read this last section. Here, you're going to identify the ways in which you motivate yourself. What does spur you into action? Take a moment to think about a time when you got off your backside and got stuck into achieving something …

How do you motivate yourself to actually do something? What works for you?

- *The desirability of the outcome?*

- *Because you want to get away from a situation you don't like?*

- *Maybe other people were urging you, or even threatening you with dire consequences if you didn't? Who acts as a motivator for you?*

- *Or maybe you just flipped a coin and went with the decision.*

Things to think about for Part 3: The Future

1. *What does success look like to you? How do you describe what the world would look like to you if you were able to change your past and move in a new and more positive direction - if you became unstuck?*

2. *What steps are you willing to take to change your present state of existence and achieve a successful behaviour change?*

3. *What steps are you not willing to take to change?*

4. *Once you achieve what you define as success, what do you plan to do to maintain your success and continually improve yourself?*

Part 4: The Cards – How to achieve the change you want

"To boldly go …"

Star Trek

"You never change things by fighting the existing reality.
To change something, build a new model that makes the existing model obsolete."

Buckminster Fuller

Overview

Achieving change requires action on your part. Thinking will not make it so. As previous attempts have failed, doing more of what you know hasn't worked, or doing it harder, is not a sensible strategy. You need to do something different.

The process you are about to undertake is essentially about constructing the world you want to live in. This world will not come out of thin air but out of the preparation you have already made in reading and working through the earlier sections of this book.

You are going to build your world in relation to your current self, holding in mind what you have said you want in Part 3. You have been thinking about the various bits and pieces of your life and who you are – some good, some not so good. You have, unconsciously, organised your life in a particular way, using stories that define who you are. Unfortunately, some of these stories are past their sell-by date, and this has led to you now feeling stuck. So if your stuckness is based on those stories, then it's these stories that need to be changed, made obsolete, deleted or rewritten because they are somehow getting in the way of you making a change.

Because this is all inside your head, it's difficult to get an objective view of it. There's too much information and everything is muddled up in there. Your working memory is limited (that's the bit of your mind with which you are currently thinking and remembering); it can't hold everything at once. That makes it hard to see the big picture, and a challenge to find your direction in the external world. Having to rely on your working memory alone creates tension, because you might forget.

The solution? Think of it as downloading what's in your mind. You're creating an objective view of your reality. You start the process of untangling your thoughts, memories, plans, ideas, and so on, by writing all of these notions on separate cards. And then, with the cards out there in front of you, your story is revealed. That makes it easy to change. Then you develop a new story, one that leads towards what you want. Being a story, it will clarify the steps needed to achieve it.

The Process

The process that follows is an effective way of working with change. At first its power may not be obvious. So what makes it special, what makes it work? The key factor is that you take what's inside and put it out in front of you; you literally gain a new perspective on the issue. This allows you to be an observer of your own experience, more realistic about it.

In practical terms, you write key words or phrases on cards, and then arrange them to show the story you are telling yourself. This is your stuff, and you will know how it all fits together. Because it's on cards, it's flexible. You can easily rearrange the cards to tell a different story. And that's the second thing you'll be doing. But first you need to write down these key ideas on cards and put them out on the table in front of you, so that you can see what you have. This is probably something you have never done before.

Preparation

Some preparation is required. You will need:
- A place for doing this, preferably a room where you can shut yourself away, and which contains a table or large flat surface, free of clutter.
- You will need to acquire, or find, a pack of blank filing cards, minimum size: standard credit card, optimum size: 110 × 80 mm or 5 × 3 inch index cards. You'll need quite a few, so be generous to yourself and have at least a hundred to hand. A marker pen for writing on the cards, in big writing, so that you can see what you have written when you're standing back, a couple of metres away.
- No interruptions, so switch off your mobile and anything else that could intrude, all those things which your mind takes an active interest in.
- Important: tell those people around you that you are going to be busy for a while, and other than real emergencies, you do not want to be disturbed.

This process will take about an hour or so – it depends – so make sure you don't have a pressing engagement for a while afterwards. It will also take more than one session. It's up to you how often you go through the process but the more times the better it will be.

You may find that using the cards becomes a regular occurrence.
- Some people like to have music in the background while they do this. Probably best to choose music that will raise your mood, keep you feeling positive, alive.

In addition, you will need:
- All your thoughts, notes, ideas, arising from reading the first three parts of this book.
- Your intuition.
- To be in a good state.

By now you should be raring to go, really keen to sort things out – at last. Of course there may be a tiny sense of reluctance, based on embarrassment or fear. That's natural. It's something new, unknown. Once you get into it, these feelings will soon pass.

It's best to arrive fresh, with a clear head, rather than one influenced by alcohol or recreational drugs.

Optional
- A trusted friend – if available. This friend is there to support you in the process, but will not interfere. They are definitely not there to advise you. If you're really stuck, they can tell you what to do next, and assist you in the mechanical parts of the process. Most of the time, though, they will be leaving you to get on with it by yourself.

Ready to begin?

Step 1. Write on the cards

Get your pack of blank cards and a marker pen. Get comfortable, and recall all the ideas that came up while you were considering your life earlier, about where you are and what you want to be different. Choose a key word for each of these things, and write that down on the cards – in big enough writing so that you'll be able to read it from a distance. Later, you'll need to literally stand back to get perspective on what you have on the cards.

This is off-the-top-of-the-head stuff – just write, don't spend a lot of time thinking. One idea will trigger another, so write down what comes. And keep on going. Even after you think you're done, there will be some more words that come to mind.
- What else? What have I missed? What needs to be there?

> Survey your life as it is now, with all your plans, your wishes, your resources, the stories that fill in the details of your life.
> - What do you want? What do you want your life to be like?
> - If you're going to be successful, what would that look like? What evidence would there be?
>
> Here are some examples of the kinds of things people write on cards:
> - People. Places. Projects. Plans. Possibilities. Names. Dates. Times. Deadlines.
> - Work. Job. Role. What gives you pleasure. How you will earn money.
> - Qualifications. Interests. Hobbies.
> - Wants. Needs. Options. Things to avoid. Side effects. Consequences.

Keep writing down what comes, in the order it comes. You are not sorting at this stage, just gathering material. Spend some time doing this; the plan is to get as much as possible downloaded so that you can see what's going on.

> Here's a piece of advice: Don't put artificial barriers in front of yourself.

There is a natural tendency to self-censor, but there is no need for this. You're the one who needs to gain clarity, so there is really no point in hiding anything, or being shy or embarrassed. If an idea pops into your head and your immediate response is "No, I shouldn't write *that* one" then that's one you definitely should write. Self-censoring is a waste of time. You are doing this because you want and need to be honest with yourself. So write down those first thoughts – the ones you usually quickly move on from to something more 'acceptable' to other people.

Have faith that 'clearing the attic' in this way is going to have a beneficial effect, and rest assured that there will be no problem in filling the attic up again. The mind does not like gaps.

You should end up with a stack of 40–80 cards. Any fewer, then you must be kidding yourself!

The Cards

Each card represents one idea that you have about yourself. You could think of it as an 'icon' as on the screen of a computer or mobile phone. You click on the symbol and it opens up into a folder or document. Or you could see it as the title of a book or a movie, a story, a song or an image.

If you feel sensitive about something, you simply choose a word that has a meaning for you and you alone. These are your codes, shortcuts, so only you will know what they mean. Well, actually, all the words we use are like this – they all have a special meaning for us. Even though we might think that other people will know what our words mean, we are often wrong. A single word is in effect the title of a complete story you have running in your life, and only you know all the details. No one else would ever know in detail the experiences that these words refer to.

Your life is a story that has yet to be told. What you have so far are the stories you have been telling yourself about who you are and perhaps the meaning of your life. These stories have definitely changed over the years, especially since your childhood. But they are just stories, just versions of your reality, neither fixed nor written on tablets of stone. Your life isn't finished yet, not by a long chalk; each moment you are adding experiences. It may be easy to ignore this *now* moment, but you never know how it will feed into the story at a later date and influence it for good or for ill. Because of your current desire for change, it would be true to say that the best is yet to come. So get rid of any ideas about permanence; the process you are going to go through next will engage you in revising, rewriting, retelling some of those old stories, and it'll be an opportunity to create some new stories that will carry you through the next stage of your life. Your new story is there to motivate you to take action. However, once you do, your life will change, and you will need to revise your goals.

Step 2. Shuffle the cards

Once you have your stack of cards with words on, your next task is to shuffle them. This simple act of shuffling the cards is a key part of this process. Shuffling eliminates any kind of pattern that arose in the thinking/writing process. Shuffling introduces a 'random' element, and thus forces you to reconsider how you think about what you want to change.

The main reason for shuffling the cards is to frustrate the 'inner librarian' (the part of your unconscious mind which seeks order and stability, and who always puts things back 'where they belong'). This aspect of your unconscious is there to defend and protect you, and tends to resist change. That's why just thinking about a change you'd like to make is unlikely to happen – your librarian wants to keep things neat and tidy.

Once you have had a good shuffle, you are going to place the cards on the table in front of you, one at a time. This is where your intuition comes in as you decide where to place each card.

There is a best way to do this:
- Lay the cards out on the table in a grid pattern (in neat columns and rows, not scattered) – make sure they're all the right way up! – and begin to impose some structure.
- To help the structuring, get a couple of cards – a different colour would be good – and write "PAST" on one and "FUTURE" on the other. A useful plan is to have the Past (which is actually your Present State) on the left, and the Future – your Desired State – on the right.

Imagine you are creating the kind of storyboard they use for putting movies together. These consist of a series of key images which show the logical flow of the story naturally moving from left to right.

- You'll know roughly where to place each card. Most of the cards you will be able to sort according to whether they relate to something in your past which has happened and gone; or are about your wishes, your outcomes based at some future time. There's third possibility, those things which are right now – and these go in the middle, right in front of you. Remember that nothing is fixed; you can adjust things whenever you like.
- As you continue to sort, you will find some themes emerging.
- Keep the grid tidy. If in the process of doing this, you think of something you wish to add, just write it on another card, and place it where it needs to be.
- However, you cannot take off a card unless you replace with a card which 'fixes the problem', so to speak. You cannot simply remove a card. Any deep negatives must be 'cancelled out' by adding another card saying what you will do instead. You have to deal with it, because the card represents some aspect of your world. What would solve the immediate problem for this card? Once you have a solution, write a new card and put this on top and add these to the new strategy/story. The original is still there, but its value has lessened.

Check that the story now flows better.
- Once all the cards are down, stand back and look at what you have.

So do that now. Create this array of cards so that you can see them all together. View the cards as: "How I construct my life".
- Where is Now? Where is the separating line between the Past and the Future?

Typically, about 90% of the cards relate to the Past: who you have been, who you used to be – rather than who you want to become. Treat the Past as things that have happened that you choose not to condemn yourself to relive every day.

Become an observer of your own process

The advantage of using the cards is that they become a kind of diagnostic tool, especially handy for diagnosing someone else. Because you have achieved this separation – you and your thoughts – it makes you the person who is doing the diagnosis. The person benefitting from this also happens to be you. And being the diagnostician, you are not going to put up with any 'excuses' for how you got to be the way you are now.

- When you look at the story you have created on the table, who does it say you are?
- Notice what's different now. It could be that things are in clearer focus, or the colours are brighter – whatever. Have your feelings changed?

There is no need to do anything other than observe these things.

- Notice if there is some kind of 'editor' or 'librarian' who pops up who wants to take control over the story, who has opinions about the way it ought to be? If so, deliberately frustrate them by taking another step back and so distance yourself from that kind of interference.

When you begin to see a new story on the table, it's tempting to start 'adjusting' it, comparing it with the old one. Resist this. Your brain can do this perfectly well without any conscious interference. Take a break – go and have a cup of tea or coffee. You might even want to sleep on it.

When you come back, if it helps, turn on your music.

Step 3. Observe

Look at the story of your past

Look at the cards on the left side of the table.
- Which are a little less helpful?
- Which have been holding you back?
- Which are based on other people's 'oughts' 'shoulds' and 'musts'? – wherever they came from: childhood, parents, school, significant others.

Childhood memories to be left behind

Some people think they had a perfect childhood; others think their childhood was either missing, or disgraceful, violated, or even not worth remembering. Whatever. It's easy to be biased, to look through rose-tinted glasses, and pick out the warm summer days, and suppress the rest. But even though your childhood wasn't perfect, it was yours. Nostalgia can be wonderful, but it is usually somewhat biased towards the positive. This is one of the times where an outside view is desirable. Someone to challenge your memories for their veracity, to ask you what happened on the drear days of boredom, or anger, or fighting.

Every childhood has its dose of fear; it's part of growing up, of not wanting to stay safe. Some fears can be left behind; you can let go of those that led to hurt. Others may be motivating even now. You need to harness such stimuli because you will continue to need their protection.

So look again at what you want, and not at what you don't want. It's time to let go of blankeys, all those blankeys that you sewed into your protective quilt – that place where you hid when things were not going how you wanted them to.

Therefore, when you notice any cards or stories that remind you of that younger you, some deeper probing may be a good idea. Assume that every behaviour has some positive intention, and that whatever you were doing in the past, it was an attempt to achieve a positive outcome – perhaps to become safe, to protect yourself or others, to survive. Think back into that story and ask yourself:

- What was my intention then? What did I want to happen? What did I want other people to do?
- And why did I want that? Why was it important?

If your new story is going to become reality, what has to die?
- What will you have to leave behind?
- You're going to become an Ex– whatever it was
- You are losing an earlier 'fantasy' self – an 'ideal' which was not realised. "The person whom I could have become *if only* …" That's something that needs to consigned to the bin.
- What of your past do you want to take with you?

And check once more:
- Is that going to work in your new reality?

Step 4. Decide which cards to keep

Split the cards into two types:
- These things I can now let go of. Some cards easily fall into the category of 'What's past is past'. You've dealt with these things, they are not longer an issue. Finito.
- Those cards which refer to things in the past which are no longer relevant, or are simply just things that happened some time, and which you no longer need, you can stack them, and put the PAST card on the top of the stack. You know those things are still there, but you don't need them for creating the future you want.

Then there are other cards which are still current, the 'unresolved' issues. Now you have to decide:
- What is salient? What's worth keeping? These are the things I must do to move into the future.
- What really needs to be let go of? Do I really need that in my life any longer?
- Are there any parts of the story you are simply hanging on to just because they were your past? Think about this: if you continue to hang on to them, you'll end up with the same old story, and nothing will change. That's not what you want.

> There is a tendency (without realising you're doing it) to find justifications for 'what always happens'. The old behaviour lives on by reinserting itself into the future, because you 'know' your dream will never work.
>
> Develop some childlike innocence: "What would it be like if I didn't know I couldn't do it?"

- What was the good that came out of what happened? What did you learn? What life experience that was valuable to you later, or now, or will be in the future?

You always have a choice. You can choose to change the polarity of such stories, or simply rub them out because they no longer serve you.

- In other words, what resources do you have that will continue to support you?

If they're not already on the table, write some new cards with these resources on.

> Extract the goodies from your past; whatever happened there was something to be learned. This may be the first time you're considering this. For example, you learned to be strong, to stand up for yourself, to not buckle under pressure. It's important you benefit from your 'mistakes' so that you won't make similar errors in future. (You'll increase the probability of this happening if you imagine an alternative scenario where you engage in a more positive response.) So look at the cards and decide which aspects of those particular stories you need to retain because they'll be useful for the future. And get rid of everything that no longer validates you now.

You can take cards off the table but it is important to replace them with an action, a 'doing' that will mean you don't repeat the old behaviours. The cards need to represent a mental map that you feel comfortable with. In fact, you need to be totally convinced you have the answer. If not, go back to the cards and keep working with them. You will know when the plan is right!

When you think you're done, for now, take a step back. Take a break.

Finding the Story

Leave all the cards visible. (If you don't remember what a card means, then either rewrite it, or discard it, and replace it was something that does mean something.)

On the Left:	I know what I've got
Towards the centre:	Things I want
On the right:	How I'm going to achieve them.

When you were arranging the cards, you were intuitively telling a story that builds on the past and extends into the future.
- What strikes you about this arrangement?
- Does it seem feasible?
- Is it a true reflection of what you want?
- Are you holding back? Is there something obvious which you've missed?
- Which cards could be somewhere else?

Look at the cards on the left. Notice where the PAST card is. You are going to move it towards the centre of the table to indicate that you have moved on. Just check in:
- How am I now?

Which makes more sense:
- Believing that the past is real?
- Believing that the future is possible to achieve?

In creating the story your present state is based on the past. So it's no longer present, and something you can dispense with. So move the PAST card to the centre, rather than stay stuck in the past. Where are you in current reality. Is the Past stuff still relevant?

Look at the cards on the right, those that relate to the FUTURE. (Sometimes you need to give yourself permission to look forwards, to get a sneak preview – remember the cinema metaphor in Part 3?) Does the future now seem nearer? Or does it seem bigger? Would it make sense to move the FUTURE card?

Look at the new arrangement, and consider:
- How has that changed things?
- How could it be even better?

Remember, you're just looking, not trying to fix anything. This is the first time you've seen your life spread out in front of you like this. Resist the temptation to try to manage it.

> If you are doing this with a friend, now would be a good time to have them watch you, only assisting when you get stuck. What would they need to ask you if they saw you were stuck? "What are you not considering?" "Is there something else about this which you're missing?"

Look again:
- What are you *not* noticing?
- Is there a place on the table you prefer not to look, or where you look away from?

Take on the role of someone who sees the world differently from you. For example: a newspaper reporter, a detective, an interior designer, a photographer, an actor, or a crime scene investigator …
- How would they see things differently? What would they pay attention to? What's important to them?

Notice any snagging points. Do you find your eyes drawn to one card? Or perhaps you are deliberately averting your gaze:
- Is there one card that embarrasses you or creates self-disrespect?

If so, then keep that one card – put it up on the mirror, or somewhere you will see it often.

Look once more:
- Which cards or card stands out as your reason for doing this process?
- One card above all is your motivator. It offends your laziness and you may pretend it's not there – it becomes an elephant in the room.
- Once you recognise the elephant, that's the way to go, you must take action there.
- Where's the best place to put the key cards?

When you adjust your priorities, how does this change the story?

> If you are working with someone else, and they are asking you these questions, bear in mind that when someone says "I don't know" that really just a place-marker, a pause while they gather their thoughts, and it is a vital space in which they need to do some more work.
>
> Don't interrupt a 'don't know' – they need to go there, without an excuse for copping out.

There is no minimum or maximum number of cards, but ideally, getting the remaining cards down to 40 or 50 cards or less makes life a lot more streamlined. Next you are going to tell the story, so you want a tight plan, but all encompassing.

Step 5. Tell the Story

Now you're going to do something different. The cards have presented you with a new structure to your reality, and a plan emerges as you see the cards in a new way. You are going to tell this story by looking at each card in turn and describing what you will be doing. By reading it out aloud you are maximising sensory input. This is a multi-mode process to enhance your understanding of yourself. You could think of this reading as telling your story to an interested listener, someone who wants to know you better. Treat this process seriously, so that means overcoming any initial embarrassment, or hesitancy. Be real, be genuine: tell the story.

> ***Storyboarding***
> Creating the story with image by image detail enables you to check the coherence of your story, and to find out ahead of time whether your plan of action will work. You don't need to wait until you do it for real. As you follow through each step, you'll soon find out if it actually works. You'll spot short-cuts, cheats, fudges and when you're not being realistic. It's no good trying to skip over the difficult bits – "and then I'll have lots of money" or "then we'll live happily ever after" – that's not going to work.

When you find a glitch, refer back to the array of cards: which card is the one that needs your attention? Which is blocking the flow? What's missing? You may need to move things around a bit.

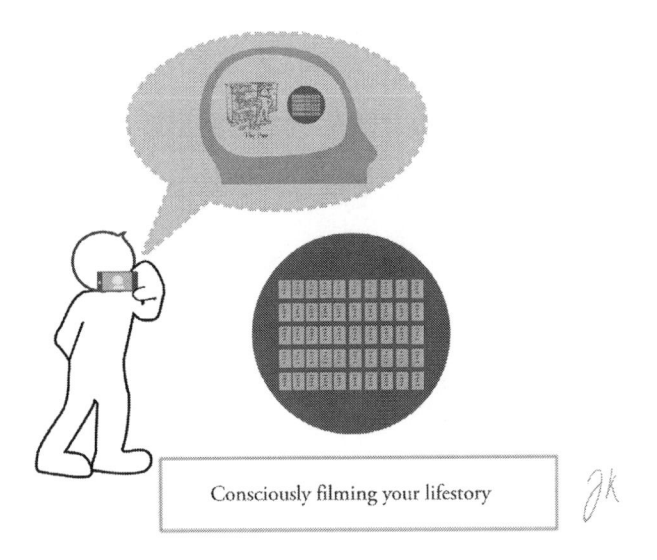

Consciously filming your lifestory

You will need a mobile phone with a video function, or a camera that takes video. Using this, you are going to narrate the story on the cards, moving one card at a time.

- You are going to start at the beginning, on the left, and you are going to get the camera nice and focused on each card in turn, showing the whole card, just that card. You are going to say out loud what that card means and how it fits into the overall story. Then you will move on to the next card in the sequence, and so on for all the cards on the table. You are telling the story in such a way that it flows by linking each card to what came before and what comes after. Keep it flowing; your video should last no more than 4 minutes – you are not recounting *War and Peace*! There's no fun in boring yourself to death by video. Keep this process totally up beat by talking as if you are already becoming a success.
- Be aware of your voice quality as you say out loud what comes to mind. When it's right, your voice changes, becomes more authentic, more resonant.

If you find it gets you across the embarrassment threshold, just pretend you believe yourself, again, keep faking it, use your most confident voice. Use words that are oriented towards the future and talk about your drive and enthusiasm. Be very mindful of the words: I can, have will, am, will etc.

If it's not working for you – if it feels shallow, false – then go back and find the reason, the Why. Is there a sticking point? Which card is holding you back?

If you don't want to move forward, you'll find an excuse – and that's a learned strategy.

Once you've sorted this, do the whole narration again, this time with more passion.

Then take a break. You need one. Go and do something else for a while.

When you come back, put on a headset (this makes it more immediate) and listen to what you have recorded and watch the images. As you are hearing yourself talk about the journey you will know whether what you are telling yourself is convincing or not, whether you are 'buying in' to it. If it doesn't flow, go back and re-read it.

> Can you fake sincerity? It's not easy. But it is easy to spot it when it's there. No one is going to beat you with a big stick if it's not quite genuine. Just make sure you're speaking from the heart.

Take off the headset. Have a break, a chance to let this experience sink in.

You may find that in making the video of the cards, you have naturally moved the story on. It's already changed. Therefore the story needs updating.

Step 6. Is that it?

Well, not quite. You have now covered the initial stages of this change process. But it's not a once-and-for-all-time event. I recommended that you watch the video multiple times. Every day. Seriously. Listen to the story, after all, it is your story, now.

As you do this, you will notice that your original story is becoming even less relevant, because you have made the change inside. Your story is fluid because life is constantly changing.

You have now done something different, and there will be consequences. Remember that when you walk out into the world afterwards, it will be unforgiving; there will be many 'forces' acting upon you trying to return you to your previous position.

Looking on the positive side, your future is now potentially richer. It's better to think of your life's journey, not in terms of length, but in terms of its richness, its density, its quality.

You may want to continue straightaway – you're firing on all cylinders. But on the other hand, you may be feeling a bit low, or desolate on the first evening after doing the process. Expect this – you've been busy rewriting your life – and your Inner Librarian is likely to be very tired having not been able to function as usual. Again, this is not an excuse for beating yourself up … that's something you no longer need to do, you know it doesn't get you anywhere. Take more control of the state you are in. Stay buoyant, stay light. Use music to keep up your spirits. Remember the positive reason why you set out on this journey. It was to do something quite special, to consciously build the life you want, the one you both desire and deserve!

Step 7. Next Time

You have found that the original story is out of date – the world has shifted, you've moved on. Now you need to rewrite the story. Do the whole process again within a week. You need time between the exercises to absorb what has happened – and this is not a conscious process. The second time you do the cards, it can be much quicker. In general, people know what's congruent about the story they have just told themselves, and what is not congruent. So you know which 'bits' to work on now – those are the bits that seemed a bit phoney, or where you got irritated with yourself.

Each time you return to this process, things will be different. If you are going to create a journey, a to-do list, a route-map to where you want to be … you will probably need to add more cards.

- What are you adding in?
- What's no longer of such importance?

Keep moving the cards, and remake the video.
- How is your story changing?
- Listen to your own voice – is it changing, becoming more authentic?

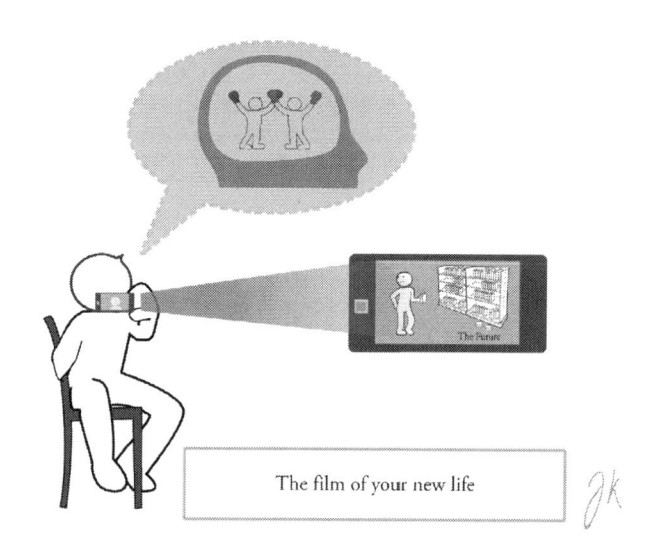

The film of your new life

Testing your work

It's important to test your plan, your journey, frequently as you go along: Is this going to work? Am I going in the direction I want to go?

It's also important to know when to exit, to know that you have arrived. This is why you set some criteria earlier on so that you would know when you have achieved what you said you wanted. It could be that now you have got there it's not quite right. That's OK. Go back and re-decide. You're in control here. Do it again. If you don't like it, it may be because it's different – this is the new you, and it will feel strange for a while. Give it a chance to become the new norm. If after a few days you decide it really isn't for you, go back and do the process again.

Ann's story continued

We met Ann in Part 1 struggling to justify her place in the management team at a recruitment agency. Ann found that the story she had been living was based on 'rules' about how to behave that she had learned in her childhood.

After working with the cards, she clarified her desire to act as 'the adult in her world'. Now, back at her workplace, Ann has noticed some very significant developments. She says that the real change was that she wasn't actually scared of them anymore. And that makes a huge difference in how you relate to others. Consequently, her staff talk very differently with her, because she was no longer shying away from conflict and hard decisions.

When Ann first returned to her company she said that watching her video became almost a daily ritual. It was her way of setting herself up for the day, and that if the wheels came off she would go into her office and watch it again to remind herself.

Last time we spoke, Ann said that she regularly updates the video in between our sessions as she has noticed this helps her to see the positive changes as they happen. She then feeds that back into her story of the life she is now leading.

Taking the first step

"But just talking about what to do isn't enough. Nor is planning for the future enough to produce that future. Something has to get done, and someone has to do it."

Pfeffer & Sutton

It's a story; it's not yet action. Sure, you have changed, and the world around you has changed to some extent. Your new story can never be a substitute for action. There is a phrase – the 'knowing-doing gap' – which has come out of management training and is relevant to change in any situation. This is the difference between knowing what to do (this is where you are comfortably 'at home' thinking about what you could do) and actually getting off your backside and doing it (starting the journey into the unknown – because even though you have storyboarded it, that does not guarantee that events will actually happen according to your scheme).

So far, everything that has happened has taken place in your room, your private space. What's in your mind is just a plan. The next step is to realise that plan by actually doing something in the world that you wish to change.

Therefore, you need to address how you are going to take action:

What is the first step?

You should by now have in place the criteria for taking action. The story should be sufficiently motivating for you to do something, do something different.

- Remember your motivating triggers? You explored them at the end of Part 3. They could be useful.

Things to think about for Part 4: Action Plan

1. *Now that you have 'laid out' your cards and have an idea of what behaviours you need to exhibit to achieve your success, what will you do to maintain your success?*

2. *Who will you include in your continuous improvement plan to help with your journey?*

3. *What will you do if you start to feel stuck again?*

Conclusion

"Live Long and Prosper"

Star Trek

Well done, for working your way through this process using the cards. We hope that you have gained what you wanted. And that you now have a practical way of working towards further goals.

In the process of reading the book and carrying out the process, you'll have realised that:
- It does demand that you are honest with yourself.
- That the more you put into it, the more you get out of it – like many other things in life.
- That it would probably work better if there was some knowledgeable person there to help you when you were unsure what to do, when you were not digging deep enough, and who could see what needed to happen when you could not.

That's why you need other people's insights ...

This isn't a one-off. You need to practise a continual conversation with yourself about where you are, how you're doing, where you want to go next. Life is about checking – from time to time – whether you are on track, are you getting what you want, what you're meant to be doing?

You will find that when you watch the video you made of the cards, you and the world around you will have changed to some extent, and that the story is showing signs of obsolescence. When you notice this happening, you need to re-do the cards – adding in new ones, removing old ones – and make an updated video which accurately reflects how you are now.

Where next?

Now that you have had an experience of using the cards, this process becomes yours.

These things you learned you will have as resources for your future.

It's yours to play with, to work with – it's on the table. It's simple and portable, and now it's up to you what you use this for.

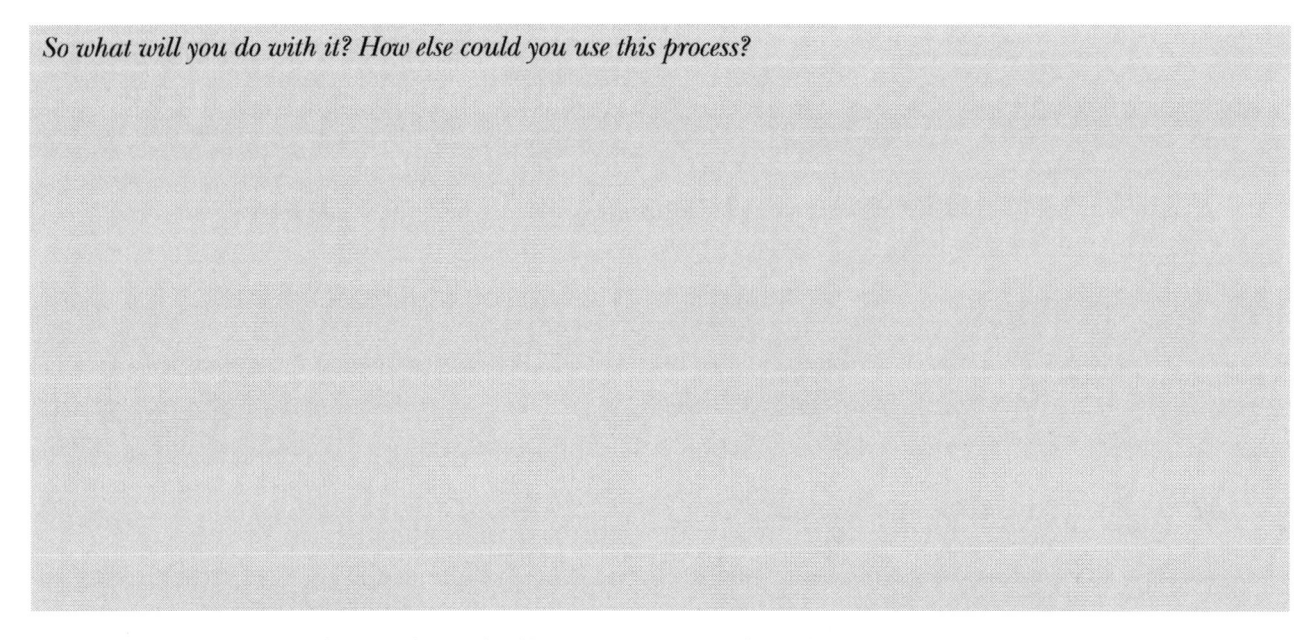

So what will you do with it? How else could you use this process?

The more you use the cards to clarify your way out of stuckness, you will find numerous applications of this simple practice of using the cards to see things from a different perspective, as observer.

There are no limits other than those you impose on yourself.

Finally

Having engaged with this process, the second question that you ask is, "If you were on your deathbed, after living your entire life, and you are going to give one piece of advice to your favourite niece or nephew who is standing at your bedside in tears, what would you say to them?

- Now take the first question that you asked yourself in the Introduction and answer it with the second one.

References

Books

- Oettingen, Gabriele (2014) *Rethinking Positive Thinking: Inside the new science of motivation*, Penguin Random House.

- Pfeffer, J & Sutton, R (1999) *The Knowing-doing Gap: How Smart Companies Turn Knowledge into Action*, Harvard, Harvard Business School Press.

Websites

1. http://calnewport.com/blog/2014/11/11/warren-buffett-on-goals-if-its-not-the-most-important-thing-avoid-it-at-all-costs/
2. http://www.ted.com/talks/ben_saunders_to_the_south_pole_and_back_the_hardest_105_days_of_my_life#t-984793

Contact details

Richard Elwell is the founder and director of Ethical Influence.

You can contact Richard at
    www.ethicalinfluence.co.uk
    email: sales@ethicalinfluence.co.uk

    Richard has been trained in many processes of developmental change. An NLP Business Master Practitioner, his thirst for new and exciting breakthroughs never ends. Everything about Richard's diverse journey has been centered on understanding the core reasons of how true change happens for people, and how these changes can become permanent. His training includes The Alternative to Violence Project; Salad Ltd's Hypnosis Training; NLP Business & Master Business Practitioner courses; MBNLP High Performance Coaching; Training Mastery-Workshop Development... the list goes on! Richard's dedication to invest in himself and his clients never ends. He totals 16 years training and continues CiPD.

    Following business stints in America, India and Kuwait Richard co founded Ethical Influence to continue excelling in the work he has always enjoyed - enabling and empowering individuals, teams & organisations. Richard works across numerous sectors and is available for keynote speaking.

Notes

Notes

Notes

Notes

Notes

Notes

Notes

Notes

Notes

Notes

Notes

Printed in Poland
by Amazon Fulfillment
Poland Sp. z o.o., Wrocław